Buddhism

and

Bumps to Babies

A celebration of personal victories by Nichiren Buddhist members

"... the journey from Kamakura to Kyoto takes twelve days. If you travel for eleven but stop with only one day remaining, how can you admire the moon over the capital?"

— GOSHO: LETTER TO NIIKE (WND1 :145, P 1027)

With deepening gratitude to:

- Our mentor, Daisaku Ikeda, third President of the Soka Gakkai International. Thank you for daring to have a vision of millions when only few were in sight. Your ceaseless efforts to empower and awaken human beings to their fullest potential has triggered a clarion call in hearts across continents to challenge and transform stubborn karma, instead of being overwhelmed by it.

- The countless Nichiren Buddhists, who in their capacity as leaders or members, work genuinely to inspire others through personal example - you are creating an endless continuum of joy and victory. Your energy and electricity are affecting eternity.

- The wonderful friends in faith who contributed their experiences and made this book a reality. Thank you for carving out the time despite having such busy, challenging lives. Thank you for being with me on this journey.

- My husband, Rohan, for holding my hand through giggles and gales. And my mother, Vijaya, for her one million daimoku campaign towards expanding our family. Thank you for believing.

  -   Neha Dutt.

Preface

The essence of Buddhism is the conviction that we have within us, at each moment, the ability to overcome any problem or difficulty that we may encounter in life; a capacity to transform any suffering. Our lives possess this power because they are inseparable from the fundamental law that underlies the workings of all life and the universe – the all-pervading law of cause and effect.

Nichiren, the 13th-century Buddhist monk upon whose teachings the SGI is based, awakened to this law, or principle, and named it "Nam-myoho-renge-kyo." Through the Buddhist practice he developed, he provided a way for all people to activate it within their own lives and experience the joy that comes from being able to liberate oneself from suffering at the most fundamental level.

This book is collection of triumphs over tribulations. It is a tribute not only to those people who have been bold enough to open up their hearts and share their private struggles and victories to inspire others, but also to life - the foremost of all treasures.

Contents

Preface 5

Andreea's Experience 7

Austin's Experience 11

Céline's Experience 13

Jemilah's Experience 16

Kathryn's Experience 23

Kris T's Experience 27

Lily's Experience 29

Mridula's Experience 32

Neha Budhia's Experience 36

Neha Dutt's Experience 39

Robyn's Experience 54

Rohan's Experience 57

Ruma's Experience 63

Seiko's Experience 72

Vidhi's Experience 76

Yumiko's Experience 81

Detailed Glossary..88

Frequently Asked Questions 99

Andreea's Experience

My husband and I have been together for almost 23 years. We met when I was just 15 and we became a couple a few years later. He was the man of my dreams. We have always had an amazing relationship. We knew we had to give each other space to grow as adults, as we met so early. We have always supported each other, no matter what. We decided to start a family quite late. We wanted to experience life before having children.

Our journey to start a family began in 2015. I was 35 at that time. We were very lucky to become pregnant straight away. I was so happy and filled with hope. We told everyone straight away, we didn't care to wait till the 12 weeks got over – we just were so happy. We were both on top of the world and everything seemed to finally click, at all levels in our life. During the 11th week of my pregnancy, we did a scan which revealed that the baby was very sick. She had very unusual physical abnormalities – her chest did not seal as it should have done, so all her organs where outside her body.

I was in shock. I couldn't believe that my baby was sick. I couldn't understand what was happening. I thought, 'what is the probability of this happening?' I had never heard of this before. I just felt that as long as her heartbeat was strong, there had to be a reason for this baby to live. Mother Nature deals with pregnancies that are not ok through miscarriage, and because I did not have one, and she was still growing in me, that meant something. We had several scans after that, went to so many different specialists, and with every one of them the advice was unanimous – to terminate the pregnancy as soon as possible because she was putting me in danger and because she would not survive outside my womb.

In the middle of the second trimester we decided to terminate the pregnancy. It took 2 1/2 days to get her out of my body. At the hospital, medication was given to me to start the contractions. When she finally came out, we both wanted to see her and be with her. I felt so sad that I was not able to help her. She was clearly very sick. I held her in my arms and felt this immense grief. A pain I had never felt in my life. I wept thinking, why is this happening? Why did this happen to me? Why ME? What's the point of this? What did she do to deserve this? We named her Saloni.

Soon after I had to be rushed to the operating theatre, as I was experiencing complications.

After this tremendous loss we decided to wait to start again because we both felt we needed to heal first. This is when I was introduced by a family member to the practice of Nichiren Buddhism. I started chanting to find peace in my grief. To connect to my deceased daughter in some way.

After Saloni's passing, we started all kinds of investigations to determine if this could happen again. The coming year, we tried to become pregnant but with no success. After further medical investigations, it was revealed that my husband had fertility issues that decreased our chances dramatically of becoming pregnant. I was almost 37 years old, at the time. We therefore decided to start IVF as this could be the only chance to get pregnant. I was scared, but hopeful. I was so determined to have a child that I didn't stop to think if this would be difficult for any of us. My husband wanted to make me happy, so he went along with whatever I was willing to do. We did everything that was asked of us, even went for couple counselling prior to starting the process, as it could affect our relationship. We made lifestyle changes – took the right food supplements, lost the extra weight, did everything you can think of, just to ensure we could increase our chances of conception. That year we had two cycles of treatment, with several transfers of embryos, but none gave us a pregnancy. We also had naturally conceived once in the middle of that year, which resulted in a miscarriage.

By the end of that year we were both exhausted, emotionally and physically. We had done everything and more but were still not successful. I continued chanting to find my inner peace.

I clearly remember the day we went to Saloni's grave. We both looked at each other and just felt total surrender. We decided then to continue to try but with no expectations that we would be successful. I finally felt free. Free from sorrow, free from pain, free from judgment but mostly free from feeling insufficient – not good enough and being barren. I was in total acceptance of what would be. I knew my intentions remained to become a mother, but they did not control me. I knew I was not put through this for nothing. I knew there were great lessons to be learned through this experience. I knew that life would not end, if we could not have a baby.

For the first time in my life, I surrendered to the universe. To that power greater than me.

Saloni's short life and passing has taught me to be kind to myself. I learnt to not ask "why is this happening to me?" but instead to accept what was happening to me and then decide how I wanted to respond. Living a life with intention is very powerful and through chanting, we can get the wisdom to create intentional causes to get the effects we want.

I learned that what had happened to me, enabled me to learn how to appreciate myself. How to really love myself even if I didn't always win. I learned that in my sorrow, I could focus on other people that have gone through even tougher situations. And I didn't have to look too far for that.

When my maternal grandmother was 37, she had just become a widow with four children. Prior to that, she had lost two children - one at the age of 8 months because there were no antibiotics back then and the other baby was stillborn. I understood that whatever I had faced was nothing compared to what my grandmother had faced. She had experienced real loss, whereas I only had to win. And despite what had happened to her, my grandmother chose to be happy. The only thing I could do, was to put myself in the best position to win, to keep persevering and making the causes to win. And the effects would follow.

I began to shift the focus from my pain and chant for other's victories. And I began feeling gratitude for all I had - I had an amazing life, great husband, close family and lots of people that supported me and were cheering me on. What was I in pain for? Yes, I had experienced loss, but it had also taught me emotional maturity and the fact that one can't control everything. The only thing that you can control are your thoughts, deeds and actions - the causes you make. You can't control what people think of you or how they receive your energy. Anything you say or do gets filtered through the lens of whatever personal stuff they are going through at that moment - which is not about you.

I decided to continue to keep making causes for victory with as much emotional integrity and love as possible. To respond to the losses in my life with intelligence and love.

The following year in January, we conceived naturally. And on the 17th of September 2018 our beautiful, healthy boy Sebastien was born in London. I chanted for his safe arrival but at the same time felt total surrender throughout the pregnancy, instead of panic.

The practice of Nichiren Buddhism brought me peace within myself. It gave me the wisdom, strength and opportunity to focus each day on what really matters in my life. Family and happiness.

Austin's Experience

When we found out we were pregnant, I was in bed. I think I heard it when Robyn, my wife, told me. But it seemed a bit unreal. I was excited but then followed the fear. I'm an actor by trade, or by birth, and the coffers were low! In fact, my financial karma has always been a challenge. Practicing Buddhism for almost 11 years now, I've learnt to expect resistance or fear, and challenge it through chanting Nam-myoho-renge-kyo. My brother and sister both already have children. I felt left behind. I felt I was not ready to be a dad. I wanted to be, but having had various behavioural issues, past mistakes included, an arrest and a few run-ins with the law, I felt I was somewhat under qualified. But through chanting and developing myself, I realised that these experiences can also be beneficial and hopefully create a positive outcome in the future. I really wanted to be a dad.

As I write this, my daughter is sleeping on me. I'm blessed. Doing classes leading up to the birth are a huge benefit but having chanted to battle any fear was priceless. All the daimoku you do is like a storehouse. When the day came and Robyn went into labour, for most of the time, I felt like we were totally prepared. Yes, I was worried and yes, I was anxious but all the daimoku and Buddhist activities we had done over the years were our fuel for this most wonderful home birth, which turned out to be, quite simply, perfect. Perfect in the sense of feeling like we were in rhythm.

So many people talk of terrible birth experiences that I'm not surprised the fear factor rules. But I think even if our home birth ended up being difficult and we had to transfer to hospital, we would have been fine and dealt with it confidently due to the preparation we had made, and all the daimoku Robyn and I had done. Annie, our favourite and our most brilliant mid wife, steered us through the whole process. We had chanted to have the perfect midwife to support us and Annie, truly, was absolute proof of the power of our practice manifested in daily life. When she arrived at the house, she was a powerhouse. She remained calm and guided us throughout and gave us strength and focus when we needed it. I remember chanting when Robyn's contractions got stronger and just trusting that we would have a great birth. (Added with some Beyoncé in the background).

The classes were brilliant leading up to the birth, but I know for a fact our daimoku solidified everything and gave us the power to win. It elevated the preparation we'd done and gave us the edge we needed when it counted, the calmness.

I could see some people initially struggled when we told them we were doing the home birth. It really made me nervous when I saw that. Also, I knew Robyn did not want any medication and that it was important to her. If I was in her place, I would have taken everything I could to reduce the pain! So, I was worried for her, as I saw the pain was immense. I chanted for her to have the victory she wanted and to help her realise that!

Apart from bringing her a potato masher to clench onto between contractions, as she kept biting my hand, mostly I think I did help her. I'm in awe of what she did. But I know she has strong Buddhist faith and that encouraged me and allowed me to manifest and trust her vision. It was an incredible experience. I was also able to manifest a great job to support our life and new baby! Daimoku, chanting, is like a super fuel. It lifted us and gave us gold!

Céline's Experience

Becoming a mother has always been something that I felt strongly about. I've always worked with children. I started babysitting regularly while I was in secondary school and have worked in schools during my years as an undergraduate student. I was very fortunate to meet the practice at a very young age, in 2004, when I was a teenager. As I moved locations while practicing in the student's division and then in the young women's division, I continuously made efforts for kosen-rufu and learnt that if I wanted to build a happy life, I had to stay close to SGI members. Working alongside my SGI fellow members throughout my life was the key guidance I had received in Trets on a student's course. I was also told to chant to become the best daughter for kosen-rufu, and then when the time came, the best wife and best mother for kosen-rufu. This stayed with me and still does to this day.

I decided to chant for my kosen-rufu partner when I was 20 and received guidance that I should put all my efforts into raising my life state first and foremost. This meant for me to become happy, to be my true self, to become strong and keep advancing in my efforts for kosen-rufu. I wanted to be happy and meet a partner who would make me happier.

I met my husband for the first time in 2008, on a train. I never in a million years expected to meet my life partner on a train! My life state was so strong at that time, and to my surprise, he accepted my Buddhist practice straight away.

Fast forward a few years ahead and we got married in 2014. One of the women's division in my district who knew me well jokingly said that I'd be pregnant within the year. I truly wished for this to happen as having a family was something that I really wanted. But the unexpected happened. I started to have strong chest pains, and I would often have to come out of my classroom where I was teaching to catch my breath. I did a few trips to A&E and saw my GP on a regular basis. I knew I wanted children, but the chest pains and the heartburns were so strong that I couldn't face becoming pregnant under such circumstances. I was truly suffering. It often felt like I was suffocating. Nobody at the time could tell me what the pains were. I got told that it was IBS, but I felt deep inside my heart that something else was causing these pains. I was determined not to give up. I wanted to heal quickly and build my kosen-rufu family. I was encouraged to chant for our baby to appear at the right time for kosen-rufu. I really chanted about it, studied the Gosho and Daisaku Ikeda's guidance and attended many SGI activities at that time. I remember a specific guidance which I kept referring to whenever health issues arose: "But your faith alone will determine all these things. A sword is useless in the hands of a coward. The mighty sword of the Lotus Sutra must be wielded by one courageous in faith. Then one will be as strong as a demon armed with an iron staff. I, Nichiren, have inscribed my life in sumi ink, so believe in the Gohonzon with your whole heart" (Gosho: Reply to Kyo'o).

I took action and called a private doctor. The receptionist was my shoten-zenjin (Japanese word which means protective functions of the universe) as she told me to do a tummy scan first and arranged an appointment within the week. After my scan, the doctor found that my gallbladder was full of stones and told me that I had to be operated because there were too many. She had the scan sent over to my GP and asked for a referral to an NHS consultant who could operate on me soon. She told me to share with the consultant my wish to have a family soon; this would help speed up the process for an operation and also shorten my suffering. I truly felt protected.

In the meantime, I changed my diet to exclude all things which could harm me and dedicated a lot of my spare time to SGI activities. I also changed my job which was causing me a lot of stress to find one that would make me happier. I later found that the new job I had found was the perfect environment to have a safe and happy pregnancy. I met with the consultant a few months later. I remember chanting a lot prior to meeting him. He booked me for an operation 3 months later.

From the time I was diagnosed to the time of my operation, 6 months had passed. A lot of colleagues at work told me this was very fast for the NHS. Again, I truly felt protected. I chanted all the way throughout.

When the time came for me to have a general anaesthetic, of course I was scared, but I asked the nurse, who was holding my hand, if she didn't mind that I chanted out loud until I fell asleep. I felt embraced by her warm smile. I woke up in pain, but a reassuring one. I was healing. All had gone well. The operation happened in July 2015 and I became pregnant with my first son in September of the same year. During that time, I kept Sensei's words close to my heart on a daily basis. The following quote by Daisaku Ikeda really resonated and encouraged me: "Health is not simply the absence of illness. Real health is the will to overcome every form of adversity and use even the worst of circumstances as a springboard for a new growth and development. Simply put, the essence of health is the constant renewal and rejuvenation of life."

Our son was born in May 2016, and in December 2017 I gave birth to our daughter. As I write this experience in February 2019, I am now expecting our third child, a boy to be born at the beginning of May 2019. This means that we will have 3 children under 3 years of age. All throughout my pregnancies and through the hard work of looking after young children, I have remained very close to SGI members, making sure I attend my discussion meetings on a regular basis. I even held a guidance day session at my flat when our first son was 4 months old.

Many members and leaders within the SGI are surrounding our beautiful family. I feel that my husband and I share this amazing good fortune of having 3 children, even though we are aware of the hard work this entails. I personally feel immense joy at raising them within my SGI community and close to the Gohonzon. There are many challenges of raising young children, which could itself be shared in another experience altogether, but due to my Buddhist practice and study, and the support I give and receive, I am determined to win and face any challenge ahead. As my mentor Daisaku Ikeda says: "To face difficulties is an honour. You must not forget this."

My mission is clear: to build a harmonious family which can happily work for kosen-rufu, thereby creating a happier society! Becoming a mother has enabled me to create even more friends, many of whom which are non-members. But I truly chant and support them until I see them become happy or happier. I rejoice seeing my friends and their children being happy and do feel the honour of sharing any struggles alongside them. We learn and we grow together. We become happy together.

It is this wonderful SGI training I underwent during my youth, that enables me to encourage and support my friends and family, whether they are members or not. This, in turn, gives me the impetus and energy to create a happy life for myself and my family.

I'd like to finish with this quote from Daisaku Ikeda:
"One person's heart moves another's. If one's own heart is closed, then the doors of other people's hearts will also shut tight. On the other hand, someone who makes all those around him or her into allies, bathing them in the sunlight of spring, will be treasured by all."

Jemilah's Experience

When I became pregnant for the first time, I had been practising Nichiren Daishonin's Buddhism for 22 years. I was woken by a gentle voice that seemed to come from my heart. It said, "Would you do me the honour of being my mother?" I took a pregnancy test a few days later and it was positive. My husband and I had been married just over a year and we were delighted.

A week away from my 12-week test, I found myself wondering about the right time to let my mentor, Daisaku Ikeda, and his wife, Kaneko, know about the baby. As I walked down the street, I had a strong sense of both of them waving at my tummy joyfully.

That night, I was awoken with a feeling in my womb that the baby didn't feel comfortable. Later I went to the loo and the baby chose to leave. I was devastated but somehow, I felt that it was a happy, joint decision by my body, and the sense I had of the baby.

I chanted frantically for hours and realised that I was terrified of being a mother, having had an unhappy childhood myself, and a particularly bad relationship with my mother. The word 'mother' filled me with uncomfortable feelings.

After several months, I realised I could reclaim the word and role of "mother" and that I needn't be anything like my mother. I was away in Los Angeles at the time and my husband came to join me. We conceived our daughter on that trip. We decided that we wanted to ask Daisaku Ikeda to name her. We checked with all our family and they were happy with our choice. We were delighted that he bestowed a name on her. He also gave us a boy's name in case the scan was incorrect. He called her Akiko. Her Kanji (adopted logographic Chinese characters that are used in the Japanese writing system) is the sun, the moon and child. The meaning is child of the sun and moon: bright cheerful child. Her name if she was a boy, would have been Mitsuaki, with similar kanji. A senior leader said it is like calling someone 'Superman'. We were delighted with the names.

A huge downturn in our finances coincided with my pregnancy with Akiko and this panicked me the most. I found that I was angry with my husband a lot and we found it hard not to argue. Again, I was frantically chanting about our situation. We were looking into homeless shelters as we couldn't pay our rent. We received two crisis loans from Social Services of £15 and £20, to buy food to last us the month.

Through the panic, I chanted with deep determination to bring our daughter into a safe space. While chanting I had a realization - how could Akiko build a bright, cheerful character if her parents were constantly arguing? I realised that her name was not just a "nice" one. It was training for us to create a foundation on which she could build her character. Something clicked in my heart and we were able to stop arguing and work more harmoniously together, towards a solution.

Akiko was born on her due day: 28th April. This date commemorates the first time Nichiren Daishonin chanted Nam-myoho-renge-kyo in Japan in 1253. Brett and I were inspired and encouraged by her choice to come on that day. Akiko is incredibly proud of her birthday coinciding with such an important Buddhist anniversary.

I was graduating from a voluntary responsibility I held within the Soka Gakkai which was to support organising large meetings with a team of fellow members. I noticed that all the graduation experiences from this group centred on securing a home against the odds. I decided that I would achieve that too. That night as I sat down to chant, I was again aware of feelings of terror and unworthiness. I found it impossible to chant for a home. I remembered some guidance I had had from a leader, who said to go back as far as I needed to find a prayer that I could chant for wholeheartedly. I was unable to chant for a home, but I could chant to have the courage to chant for a home. Or the belief that I could find the courage to chant for a home.

I stumbled on a houseboat for sale for my mother who was thinking of relocating. She didn't like it, but we fell in love with it. They were asking for 50% upfront and the rest to be paid over 10 years. We made a counteroffer of 10% and the rest over 15 years and amazingly they agreed. The 10% was to come from a lump sum that my husband was hoping to achieve from an acting job. The job didn't materialise.

I returned to work when Akiko was 6 weeks old and Brett came with me so I could feed her in my breaks. My company paid for a dressing room for her to use. The protection from our faith was immense. On the first day of returning to work however, I had an emotional meltdown. I felt it was a tragedy that I had to work so soon, and that we weren't going to be able to secure the boat we were dreaming of. I couldn't bring myself to tell the current owners we hadn't found the money.

We chanted furiously again to stay united and kind to one another and the phone rang. The owners suggested that we pay them £12k for a year to see how we all felt about it and we could take it from there. Thanks to the fact that I had returned to work, and the tiny savings we had, we managed to scrape the money together. We were aboard! Our altar fits perfectly, to the millimetre, into a spotlighted alcove the previous owners designed for their TV and takes pride of place in our home.

We moved in when Akiko was 4 months old, with all our arrears cleared. The family had used a shipping company to send their possessions abroad and they had left behind the courtesy pen. The name of the company was: Seven Seas. Seven Seas is also the name of the voluntary group I was part of where I determined to secure a home when I graduated. We have framed the pen as a memento.

Also, my Aunt was the first to practice in our family. Her favourite Buddhist allegory was: The Ship to Cross the Sea of Suffering. She would chant imagining that she was at the helm of a boat containing all her family journeying to happiness. When my aunt died, we let Daisaku Ikeda know. He sent us a message: "I am sending daimoku to your aunt".

We now live on a boat as does one of her sons and my mother. Again, a cheerful happenstance from our practice. We have Buddhist activities at our home as much as possible as an expression of our gratitude for achieving a home through faith.

My husband and I had taken the fact that Daisaku Ikeda bestowed both a girl's and boy's name upon Akiko, that we were waiting for a son. We had always wanted two children. Brett is one of two and I am an only child and had always wanted a sibling. We thought it would be wonderful to have one of each, although any healthy baby was all we really wanted. Having Akiko had made us parents and she was "enough".

When Akiko was two-years old I became pregnant and we celebrated as if our family was complete. Delighted, I began the maternity support process with the GP, and we inhabited a bubble of joy. A week before my twelve-week scan the baby decided to leave. I was devastated as we had done a huge mental leap to already being the "complete" family of our dreams.

I commiserated with Brett by drinking a glass of wine and visited the emergency pregnancy unit (EPU) the next morning. The nurse who scanned me shared my

disappointment and began the ultrasound. She turned to me beaming and said, "The baby is there! You must have been carrying twins. There's a little bleeding behind the twin that is still there. But it is definitely there!"
"But I drank some wine last night!" I told her in a panicked voice.

"Don't worry," she said. "I'm sure the baby will not have been bothered by that. However, you have a fibroid the size of a five-month-old foetus which is putting a lot of strain on your womb. Please rest and try to remain positive, but it is highly likely that carrying a baby will be too much for your body until the fibroid is removed."

My thoughts rushed back to a home visit I made to a friend who had trained to be a doctor before she had a life changing brain injury. It was winter. As usual, I was wearing a cropped top revealing my abdomen. This choice of clothing was an expression of my insecurity. She gently pointed out that to be fertile, one's womb needs to be kept warm. I stored up the advice but was unable to change my style of dressing until many years later.

The second of the twins chose to leave two weeks after my visit to the EPU. The pain in my heart was so severe I felt utterly broken. The feeling that the loss was my fault was unbearable. Being strong for Akiko, delighting in her giggles and antics helped me stay focused on healing my broken my heart and to turn the suffering into joy.

The doctor who prepared me for the fibroid surgery drew a diagram of where it was situated. It was in the centre of my womb on the outside wall of my uterus. Any surgery involving the womb has a risk of creating a situation where a hysterectomy is essential for the patient's survival. The doctor explained that the chances were extremely low for me having that outcome as the fibroid wasn't inside the uterus.

I chanted to understand why my body had grown such a large fibroid which was compromising my fertility. After battling the self-loathing in front of the Gohonzon a gentle realisation came to me. The fibroid had grown in the most sensitive way it possibly could. It was outside my uterus and I was able to carry Akiko with it being present. My body had grown it to protect my womb by keeping it warm. Now it was ready to be removed as its mission to protect my womb was completed.

As I continued chanting with gratitude for the fibroid, I realised the twins' mission was to show me how much I wanted a second child and that I wasn't ready for one. I felt as though I was "cheating" on Akiko somehow. I felt that I wasn't ready to share my love and that she would find it hard too. I am so grateful to the twins for showing us so much.

Two years later, I returned home to a locked door and came in through the window. My oldest friend was looking after my daughter on the pavement. She had driven us home from an emotional lunch, where she was discussing with her closest friends her plans to move to Australia for good. I was very upset.

I misjudged my footing and fell 10 feet in high heels to the kitchen floor. As I fell a passage from Nichiren Daishonin (the founder of our faith) came up in my heart. The passage was: "afflictions of the head, eye and back are indicative of changing karma". I also heard another soft voice of determination that said, 'this has to be ok'.

My heel snapped and I crumpled to the floor. Gingerly, I wiggled my toes. I could still use my legs. Driven by the adrenaline hit, I managed to crawl to our altar, open the doors and chant with gratitude for my legs. The adrenaline passed and I crumpled back to the floor in agony.

My neighbour had meanwhile come in and taken Akiko out for a walk and my friend had called the ambulance. I was overwhelmed by a desire to move my upper back gently back and forth in a shimmy-style. The paramedics took me up the internal steps in a chair. I was allowed to go to the loo on a commode and to get myself on to the x-ray table. Soon I was in a hospital bed and was given painkillers that helped me tremendously.

The CT scan team came shortly and wrapped me in a neck brace and told me I wasn't allowed to move. The nurses and I were giggling as I had been able to move fairly freely before. The result of the CT scan showed I had broken my back and a piece of shattered vertebrae was perched on my spinal cord. Any movement could severe it and I would lose mobility from L1 down. This would be no feeling from my mid back down. My continence would also be affected, and I would be wheelchair bound.

I chanted again with profound gratitude that somehow that little shimmy must have secured the bone just enough to keep my spine intact until that moment. The paramedics could have inadvertently paralysed me by sitting me on a chair. Any position other than lying flat on my back, would have put pressure on the bone fragment and could have dislodged it. I should have been stretchered to the ambulance. Also, the use of the commode and getting on the X-ray table were moments my spine may have been affected. I had been so protected.

My surgery went well the next day. After 3 months of recovery I became pregnant with my son. Daisaku Ikeda named him: Masao. His Kanji is strong, courageous, justice and man. My husband and I again realised that this is our training – to become strong, courageous people of justice so he can build that character.

Masao was due to be born at the beginning of June. As Akiko's birthday is so deeply connected to the SGI, I found myself very attached to Masao having a birthday that was also an SGI anniversary. June 4th is Ikeda Kayo Kai day. It means flower/sun group. It is an informal training group created by Daisaku Ikeda as an invitation to all Buddhist young women to achieve happiness and progress in faith, life and peace with their family and friends by striving alongside him as his ambassadors. June 6th is the founder of the SGI, Tsunesaburo Makiguchi's birthday. I particularly hoped Masao would choose that day and became increasingly attached to this determination.

I was out walking and spotted a cloud that looked like an ultrasound of a baby. I took a photo of it to show Brett. As I did so, I had this quiet awareness that Masao wanted to come early. At my routine check-up in the middle of May, the doctors noted that my blood pressure was very high and recommended inducing me for both our safety. Masao arrived on May 20th. He and Akiko had identical births. Both delivered with ventouse and forceps. They were born in different hospitals to one another, but both were born to the same song on the radio: Christina Aguilera's 'Beautiful.' Brett and I found this amazing and encouraging.

Still I battled feeling disappointed that Masao wasn't born on a "special" day. I mentioned this to a friend who is born on the founding day of the SGI: January 26th. She encouraged me by saying that the SGI was founded three years after she was born so May 20th could be an anniversary in the future. As I continued to chant about this, it occurred to me to do an internet search to see if anything significant had happened within the SGI on May 20th.

Daisaku Ikeda visited the University of Sussex on that date, and a culture centre was opened on the same day in India. I was so moved at how prolific Daisaku Ikeda's efforts for peace are, that pretty much every day is an anniversary of him doing something significant! I understood that Masao's choice of birthday is to train me to deepen my commitment to making every day "special" by striving to win, which is a far more valuable gift from him than to have had a birthday that is already an anniversary.

Daisaku Ikeda sent us a commemorative A4 sheet for each child, with the kanji, his seal and their date of birth on it. These are framed and displayed at home. We all enjoy looking at them and draw inspiration from them. We have also framed a message he sent us: I am praying for your family's great happiness.

We are raising Akiko and Masao to have a relationship with Daisaku Ikeda through his guidance to children. We also regularly attend activities as a family. Both children consider themselves Buddhists. Akiko gave a power-point presentation to her classmates about the SGI and our faith last year. Masao was invited to speak at his school assembly when his class shared a presentation on Buddhism as part of a multi-faith week. He shared the phrase: Nam-myoho-renge-kyo with the whole school and faculty. I sincerely hope they continue to prove the power of this practice to themselves.

I am still fully engaged with my journey to live Masao's name. Whenever I am scared, which I have realised is a deep tendency in my life, I draw on his name for inspiration to break through the fear. Through chanting to overcome it I can see how both our children are living up to their names. We are so inspired by Daisaku Ikeda and his care and discernment. I feel so fortunate to have him as my mentor and to have this practice in general.

Thank you so much.

Kathryn's Experience

Since I was a young girl, the one thing I've been most excited about experiencing in life is becoming a mother. I met my partner Danny in 2009. We spent most of our relationship living together in London. I was working as a Fashion Designer, working long hours and becoming consumed about working my way up the ladder. Danny, similarly, was living and breathing work life. Family aspirations were very rarely spoken of as it seemed more important to be concentrating on 'earning money and proving ourselves on our chosen paths'. Deep down fashion design wasn't making me happy but I fought very hard at suppressing this realisation, as I think I was scared about leaving the life I'd spent such a long time working on. It wasn't until something really tragic happened to our family that I realised what is important in life.

In 2013, I lost my sister. Lynsey was my best friend, as well as my sister. Losing the person I had always looked up to and turned to whenever I was in need completely shattered my world. It was at this point in my life that things began to change. I always say that losing Lynsey completely broke my heart, but it also woke me up to life. She gave me new eyes, and a determination to become a better person.

It was around this time that I met the practice. I had chanted a few times with my brother, who had been chanting for a number of years. There was something that I felt completely drawn to with Nichiren Buddhism. Every time my brother would speak about this Buddhism, it always made sense to me.

When I lost Lynsey, I knew that I needed something to help me and I dedicated myself to chanting twice a day, every day, from that day on. I remember asking myself whether this was the right cause for me, and I asked for a 'sign' to prove that chanting was. That morning, when I got on the Northern Line tube to work, I managed to get a seat (a rarity on my commute). I dosed off as I often did, and when I woke up, the person who stood up in front of me in the aisle was reading, "An Introduction to Nichiren Buddhism'. If this wasn't a sign, I don't know what is. This felt like the universe was giving me a wave to say you're on the right path, stick with it. And I did. I received my Gohonzon in December 2014.

I knew that I had the ability to be happy despite any situation. Buddhism taught me this and chanting gave me the tools to do so. I had the choice to allow myself to suffer, or I could learn from this experience and gain strength and wisdom from it. Both of which I knew my sister would want for me.

"True happiness is not the absence of suffering. You can't have day after day of blue skies. True happiness lies in building a self that stands dignified and indomitable. Happiness does not mean having a life free from all difficulties but that whatever difficulties arise, without being shaken in the least, you can summon up the unflinching courage and conviction to fight and overcome them," Daisaku Ikeda.

Chanting gave me the strength and courage to work through what seemed like an unimaginable situation. I realised I had always been living my life in fear, not able to make decisions and take action to make change. After Lynsey passed away, I handed in my notice at work, decided to leave London, and go and travel on my own. Danny stuck by me through this choice, letting me go so I could have some space to process things.

After travelling, I decided to stay in Somerset and work on the life that felt truly important to me. And this was working on my art, being close to my family and at some point, starting a family of my own. Danny decided to move out of London too, and we set up a home together in Somerset in 2016.

At the start of 2017 I wrote down my determinations for the year ahead, something I always do in January. One of these determinations was for my body to be working, in order for us to start trying for a baby the following year. I had always struggled with irregularities in my body's cycles, so becoming pregnant seemed like it was going to be a long journey.

We were both shocked and stunned in July to find out I had become pregnant, after us not even beginning to actively try for a baby. This news brought a whole number of emotions our way - shock, excitement and fear. Danny and I both initially really struggled with getting our heads around how quickly this had happened. Both of us felt we weren't ready for it yet. Despite how much I wanted this and had done so my whole life, I was still riddled with the fear of not feeling ready for change. The initial shock took a while to sink in but after lots of chats and dialogues (and a whole lot of daimoku) this soon dissipated into complete gratitude and open arms to the new chapter that was going to come our way.

The day of the 12-week scan arrived. The journey up to the hospital was filled with conversations of names, plans and hopes for the future. We were completely heartbroken to find out, however, that our little miracle baby didn't have a heartbeat. I'd experienced a silent miscarriage. Something I'd never heard of before. I hadn't realised how common miscarriage is. We'd got so caught up in the excitement of being pregnant that we hadn't prepared ourselves or anticipated that we may lose this baby. This was a total shock and completely devastating news for us both. It took Danny and I a while to digest. We allowed ourselves space to grieve whilst also supporting one another. I knew through my Buddhist practice that I had to learn from this experience, rather than be defeated by it. I chanted to make sense of this situation and to find courage and strength to move forward and try again.

Danny and I believe that the baby we lost came to teach us a big lesson. It made us realise how much we really wanted a baby and we were 100% ready. I had to be grateful that I was able to get pregnant, something that I was really worried I might not ever be able to achieve. From that day on I chanted with the belief that I would get pregnant again and I had to be positive about this experience. I had to believe that 'Winter always turns to Spring' a Gosho I've be drawn to throughout my time chanting. Below is an extract from this Gosho:

'Those who believe in the Lotus Sutra are as if in winter, but winter always turns to spring. Never, from ancient times on, has anyone heard or seen of winter turning back to autumn. Nor have we ever heard of a believer in the Lotus Sutra who turned into an ordinary person. The sutra reads, "If there are those who hear the Law, then not one will fail to attain Buddhahood."

This quote is found in the 2nd chapter of the Lotus Sutra:

'Our constant effort to transform Winter into Spring is the essential path to achieving fulfilment and insurmountable growth in our lives.'

Danny and I started trying for a baby in the November on 2017 and were lucky enough to conceive in January 2018. To get pregnant again so quickly filled us with joy, but also wariness of the fact a miscarriage could happen again. But we remained positive and decided to just take each day as it comes and keep our hopes up. I chanted vigorously throughout my whole pregnancy. We had a couple of scares along the way, ending up in hospital for scans. I kept the faith and didn't allow these scares to set us back.

Danny also chanted with me. For the last month of my pregnancy, Danny joined in with my daimoku, every day. Danny had never chanted with me before, so I was very taken aback when he dedicated himself to do this for us. But he had watched how much this practice had made me grow as a person and how it had given me the strength to work through obstacles, throughout my life. We had a wonderful last month, chanting for a happy and healthy baby, and a positive labour, without any complications.

I was due on the 10th of October and our little girl was born on the 14th. We were lucky to have her in a midwife-led centre near our home- something both Danny and I had chanted for together. The labour was long, a tiring 44 hours long, but no intervention was needed and there were no complications. It was by far the most euphoric experience I've ever had.

I truly believe all my chanting and faith gave me the strength to get through the labour. I knew this deep down, but we had another actual proof of the practice during the labour, which confirmed both to Danny and I, how protected we were. My brother Duncan complied a playlist of music to listen to while I was in labour. The playlist had 260 songs to choose from. Both Danny and I were in complete amazement that out of all the songs on the playlist, the one our little girl came into the world to was 'Nam-myoho-renge-kyo'. This played for the last 40 minutes of my labour.

We now are enjoying family life with our little girl, Evelyn Grace, and feel completely blessed. We chant with her every day and watch how the sound of daimoku calms her.

This journey has been challenging but completely rewarding and I couldn't have got through it without my faith and hope. I know now that 'Winter will always turn to Spring'. We mustn't ever lose hope. No matter what obstacles we meet, we have the choice to remain strong. And I'm going to keep 'roaring' through life with high spirits for both my sister and our little miracle baby.

SGI President said in his novel, The New Human Revolution, "When the spring of victory comes after a winter of harsh trials, everything is transformed into happiness and joy. Without having cried, you cannot genuinely laugh; without having suffered, you cannot savour real joy. I'm sure there are times when, in the midst of some difficulties, you think, 'Why me?' But that in fact is your change to fulfil the mission you have chosen. The deeper your suffering, the greater your mission."

Kris T's Experience

My story starts about four years ago, when my husband and I decided to try for a baby. My determination was to give birth by the age of 38. I was 37 years old at that time, and healthy, or so I believed. Months passed by, without any double lines showing up and I became increasingly depressed. I took many medicines for the purpose of conception. A year later, I asked for medical help and got diagnosed with blocked Fallopian tubes. I kept chanting for miracles meanwhile, to make the impossible possible.

The first time I went through IVF, it was unsuccessful. Both my husband and I cried. We went through IVF a second time and failed. We both cried again. I was so sure I had conceived the second time, that I even made my husband believe that this time it had worked. But when my periods started, we were devastated.

After that, I decided to go through an immunology test which showed that I was killing my own baby. Normally when you get pregnant, the immune system protects the baby, however mine doesn't. It treats it as it was an invader. I accepted the fact that perhaps I would never be able to give birth. My eyes dried – I cried so much. I guess I lost parts of my soul somewhere in the process. However, through chanting, I decided that I would not give up on the possibility of leading a happy life. I am continuing to work hard to accept and still be happy and manifest my full potential and show what I am capable of!

Sometimes I still find it difficult to understand why it is so easy for some people to conceive. But I now take this road with pride! It is a very hard path, very hard. But I am glad to experience it! I guess I have always known I might not be able to give birth. I have now, through chanting regularly and being in rhythm with the practice, achieved a state of life where I am grateful for everything and everyone around me - my loving family, my friends and most importantly – my husband.

I know we have not won yet, in terms of having a family. However, we do our best to lead a happy life 'no matter what!' as Sensei says. I have overcome a lot of difficulties, sadness, hatred, jealousy, depression. I have transformed the feeling that I am ashamed of my infertility!

We are going to try twice to conceive, first with my own egg and then if that doesn't work, with a donor egg. After that, if neither attempt is successful, we will try to adopt a child.

To be fair, I would be so thrilled to have someone so precious in our lives, that it doesn't matter anymore which channel the baby comes from. We will do our best to conceive and if that doesn't happen, we will give our best as adoptive parents. It's a true liberation of this infertility prison I had put myself in!

My ultimate quote is 'Happiness is something we must create for ourselves. No one else can give it to us.' Daisaku Ikeda.

Lily's Experience

The stories we hear have a powerful impact on what we believe to be possible, especially when faced with the unknown, or areas that frighten us. In those situations, where strategy can't eradicate danger, intellect can't secure success and money can't buy peace of mind, we are left at our most vulnerable. But it's from a place of vulnerability that often we manifest the strongest faith.

I always imagined I would have children one day, and that when I did, I wanted as natural a birth as possible, and to give birth in the comfort of my own home. When I found out I was pregnant, and the prospect of childbirth loomed closer, it became increasingly apparent to me that the story our society likes to tell about childbirth is a story of horror— pain, screaming, tearing, blood —something to be survived!

But I also heard faint rumours of another tale; something beautiful, transformative, water births, home births, births that felt empowered, perhaps even magical. So, I began collecting these positive birthing stories, seeking them out from friends and family, mum chat rooms, books, podcasts.

Each time I found one, I felt a little more confident that I could have the positive birthing experience that I wanted. However, at our early scan it was noted that my placenta was lying low. If it remained in this position, it was explained to me that the baby wouldn't be able to get out and so I would have to have a caesarean. I was assured that 9 out of 10 times the placenta naturally moves out of the way by the next scan, so I didn't really worry about it as the odds were in my favour.

At the next scan however, it was still lying low. I was scheduled a further scan for two weeks later, to see if it could creep out the way, it needed to be 2-3cm clear for a natural birth to be possible. I asked if there was anything I could do to encourage it to move? Exercises? Standing on my head? Unfortunately, the answer was no.

At first, I felt powerless but then I realised they were wrong; I could chant of course! This time I chanted with confidence that the placenta would move out of the way, chanting from the point of victory that we would be in no doubt that I could go ahead with a natural birth at home.

At the next scan, the sonographer set about trying to confirm its location and joyfully announced it was now 5cm clear, over twice what it needed to be, and I was good to be signed off for a home birth. The doctor was so taken back by the radical change on my medical notes that he made me have another scan before he would believe it. Now the placenta was out of the way I began preparing for a home birth, but a midwife noted that from the scans the baby was rather large - 98th percentile in fact - with a very large head circumference. She asked me straight out if I would be able to birth this baby naturally or whether I would be better to opt for a caesarean. I was shocked. I had no idea what would be possible or not and was looking to her for reassurance, so I was suddenly thrown into a panic. Perhaps I wouldn't be able to do it, perhaps I would end up with severe tearing, incontinence, risk to my baby, or end up having a caesarean anyway.

I hoped that the baby would come soon after 36 weeks so that it could continue its growing on the outside. It didn't. At 41 weeks I was still pregnant and huge. It was at this point that I became almost obsessed with finding birth stories that could assure me that this was possible. I listened to podcasts and read far too many mumsnet chat forums, but was unable to find examples of women who had given birth at home, in water, to a big baby, with a big head circumference, with no tearing or grazing, as a first-time mum. Then my waters broke.

It was 5.30am on Sat 1st Dec. I was glad that things seemed to be moving at last, but realised I now had a new challenge to my home-birth dream. I had to be in active labour within 24 hours or I'd have to move into the hospital to be induced and put on antibiotics, as the baby would then be more susceptible to infection.

Contractions flowed steadily all day but despite my efforts to speed them up, they didn't intensify. Fifteen hours passed and my anxiety was rising as knew I only had nine hours left and the contractions were slower than when they had started. I had no more strategies to try except the Strategy of the Lotus Sutra. I got in front of Gohonzon.

As I chanted, I realised how much fear was still holding me back. I also realised I had created a barrier between me and the medical staff, as I felt like they were trying to get me into hospital and that I would need to fight them for what I wanted.

I chanted to release the fear I felt and to believe that whoever was on duty that night would perfectly support me. As I continued to chant, I realised that I hadn't really dared to chant for the birth I wanted because I was scared of being too attached to it, and therefore disappointed if complications arose. I was waiting to see proof in the outside world rather than manifesting the faith that it was possible from within. I also realised deep down that I felt selfish to chant for it because who am I to deserve something 'special'.

All these feelings came out in front of Gohonzon and as I faced them, my fear started to change to courage. I determined that mine would be the birthing story that I hadn't been able to find, and that I would be able to encourage other first-time mums with my experience. I determined confidently to have my baby in the birthing pool, in that very room, in front of Gohonzon. I then let go of any strategy and chanted to have the birthing experience that would encourage as many people as possible. As my courage grew, the sound of daimoku grew too and I turned to see my husband had sat to join me.

An hour passed in front of Gohonzon, an hour I will never forget. By the end I felt completely different and I knew I was ready. My wisdom told me that to get this labour moving I must go for a walk immediately. By the time I got to the bottom of the road the contractions had intensified immensely. I returned and repeatedly paced the length of my house, the contractions becoming progressively stronger and more frequent. A couple of hours later I rang the midwives to come. I expected they might take about 15 minutes, but due to complications of not being able to find a second midwife (you need two for home births) they didn't arrive for another two hours!

But all I cared about was the confirmation that I was in active labour, so that I could continue to birth the baby at home and when they did arrive their checks confirmed that I was 4cm dilated and most definitely in active labour! The midwife then explained that they would expect the baby to arrive in around 9 hours at midday. I listened to her incredulously, another nine hours? No way! She said they would check my dilation again at 6am to check I was progressing. She then left me and my husband in peace and went to another room to wait to be called, which was exactly what I'd wanted but hadn't even told her.

Before the next check had even come around, at 5.30am, she came back in and told me she could see the head, and to only push when my body was telling me to. And soon after, in the birthing pool, in front of Gohonzon, my big headed, 9-pound, beautiful baby boy was born. The midwives were amazed to confirm I had absolutely no tearing or grazes.

I lifted him out of the water and held him to my chest and watched him take his first breath as my husband and I chanted Nam-myoho-renge-kyo, full of gratitude, staring into his eyes.

Mridula's Experience

When I was 20 years old, I was diagnosed with a gynaecological disorder known as Polycystic Ovarian Syndrome (PCOS). Caused by stress, a common side effect of this condition is to cause weight gain and reduce fertility. At that stage, I was pursuing a highly competitive MBA programme and all I was really interested in, was building a career and earning lots of money! Finding a partner, marriage and children were far from my mind.

2 years later, I was introduced to Nichiren Buddhism by my boyfriend's mother. This beautiful philosophy of fundamental respect for life and all living beings deeply reinforced and gave a structure to my own personal values. Activities for kosen-rufu became a part of my life. I had the great good fortune of training as YWD leader, taking care of a tiny group of young women. It is truly amazing that when we moved into our kosen-rufu house, I was the only one practicing for miles. Attending my local district meeting meant I had to take the car and drive for at least 20 minutes. Today, exactly 14 years on, bodhisattvas of the earth have emerged from everywhere, and there is a large district in just my apartment block!

A few years later, my boyfriend and I got married and relocated to London. While I had to leave my job in India due to the relocation, I managed to find a great but highly demanding role, structuring and selling complex financial products. Again, babies were not on my mind! I always assumed with my PCOS diagnosis that I would require medical intervention in order to conceive. And that it would be a planned decision. So, it came as a shock when an upset stomach over a Bank Holiday turned out to be morning sickness and I found myself unexpectedly pregnant, exactly 2 months after I had been given a big promotion at work that I had chanted hard for. I felt exhilarated and terrified at the same time.

The first time I saw the tiny squiggle with a strong heartbeat beating rhythmically on the screen, I felt tears flood my eyes. I felt an enormous sense of responsibility towards this life that was now growing inside me. At the same time, I worried about being able to fulfil my responsibilities at work. I leaned heavily on the staff of Nam-myoho-renge-kyo to make my way through these unchartered waters of parenthood! President Ikeda's incredible guidance for families, especially his encouragement for mothers to be able to expand their horizons beyond their children, and to consider the workplace as a place for personal development, was deeply encouraging. In his essay titled 'The Independent Homemaker', President Ikeda writes "A working woman has the triple role of an employee, wife and mother...It is only by carrying out several roles that a person can be fulfilled as a human being. It is foolish to take the easy way out and deny oneself access to the enjoyment of one's full potential."

Of course, actualising this in life requires a lot of hard work and a lot of daimoku to support it! My daughter was born on a Monday evening, and by Friday night I was ready for a break - except, as I realised with a sinking heart, there was no break and no weekend. Seen through the long tunnel of retrospection, that first week seems comical in the feelings that it engendered in me. Although at that time, it was anything but funny. And as a cherry on top, a few weeks later, I was also asked to take responsibility for my local district.

My first instinct was to refuse, wondering how on earth I would manage work, a baby and the district. But again, I had to go back to the first principle of basing myself on prayer and chanting 'Nam-myoho-renge-kyo', to expand my life. A senior leader once said when our life condition expands, all our problems appear trivial in comparison because we are towering over them. And so it was with me - with each home visit, every daimoku campaign and every effort I made for kosen-rufu, I experienced manifold benefits at work and home.

In 2013, when my daughter was 3, we decided to expand our family. I wrote in my goals for that year, that I wanted to have a wonderful addition to our family, another fortune baby who would complete our tiny family. Given our experience the first time around, I naively assumed it would be as easy the next time around. And with every passing month, our disappointment grew.

I approached it like a work problem and assumed enough tests would solve the problem. But all that did was cause more heartache, as all the tests we did were entirely normal. However, the PCOS had returned and I was put on medication to regulate the levels of insulin in my body. More time passed, and yet nothing happened. 'Sometimes it takes time' said our understanding GP. 'But how much time is enough?' I wondered. Around this time, we also finally bought our own home in London and had a tremendous victory in finding exactly what we wanted. That year came and went, and we still had not conceived.

I realised I was not aligning my goal for expanding our family with kosen-rufu. In 2014, I made a fresh determination to expand our family, this time with the full knowledge that my responsibility as a parent was to bring up Sensei's successors - to carry forth the torch of world peace & upholding the fundamental dignity of life into the future. This became my deep prayer, for my daughter and for our next child, for both of them to understand their role and mission in life.

Finally, in August 2014, the stick came up with 2 blue lines - we felt incredibly happy. Our baby was due in early April. But that was not the end of this experience. I developed substantial morning sickness that stayed through the pregnancy. In addition, I also developed a painful condition known as SPD, in which the bones of the pelvic girdle move apart. I had had this with my daughter, and it had now come back with a greater intensity. While I was not able to participate in activities as before, I still managed to attend discussion meetings and keep up my daily practice. I used the adage that 'Buddhahood is Wisdom', to guide me and to paraphrase Nichiren Daishonin 'When Buddhahood emerges from within, it receives protection from without'.

Around December, routine blood tests showed that my platelet levels had been falling and were below normal. Low platelets can cause complications in labour, including a life-threatening condition known as HELP syndrome. 2 months prior to this, one of my closest friends, who had been pregnant with me, lost her son at 8 months. We were still reeling from the impact of this tragedy, when my diagnosis was made. While at first, we felt intensely vulnerable imagining every outcome possible, good sense prevailed. I was determined to give my baby the best possible opportunity. I stepped up my daimoku to chant for a high life condition for both of us. Every two weeks, I had to get my platelets tested, and every test showed a lower number than before.

President Ikeda has said that "The heart of the great vow for kosen-rufu and the life-state of Buddhahood are one and the same. Therefore, when we dedicate our lives to this vow, we can bring forth the supreme nobility, strength and greatness of our lives."

My parents visited us at Christmas, and we had a great holiday. On New Year's Eve, we had a Buddhist style new year's party for our district and exactly at 12:00 midnight, all the members did Gongyo together. I vowed to be in perfect health and vowed to bring forth my Buddhahood. My parents were going to come for the delivery, and I looked forward to enjoying time with my mother and father, and new baby.

Two months later, on the 2nd of March, my father had a stroke and went into a coma. Five days later, he passed away peacefully. Due to my advanced stage of pregnancy, I was not allowed to travel to India, but I managed to say my goodbyes on the phone. My mother was supported by our entire extended family, and she never had a lonely moment. I had spent each one of the five days chanting like I've never chanted before, and felt deeply connected to my father, to a point where I woke up at 6:00 am on the 7th of March, the exact moment that he passed away. Suddenly, all the events of the previous months, my friend's loss, my ill health and now my father's death seemed connected and I chanted fighting daimoku with the determination not to be defeated and not be afraid.

My mother came to London, and probably for the first time in my life, I verbalised how grateful I was to her and my dad for bringing me up to be the person I was. For always making me feel special. And in my heart, I wanted to do the same for my children.

Exactly twenty-one days after my father died, our son was born. Mystically, the final test of my platelets as I went into labour, was entirely normal. We were able to go home the very next day. We named him 'Abhay', a Sanskrit word meaning fearless.

In the Gosho, 'On Attaining Buddha in This Lifetime", Nichiren Daishonin writes "If you wish to free yourself from the sufferings of birth and death you have endured since time without beginning and to attain without fail unsurpassed enlightenment in this lifetime, you must perceive the mystic truth that is originally inherent in all living beings. This truth is Myoho Renge Kyo. Chanting Nam-myoho-renge-kyo will therefore enable you to grasp the mystic truth innate in all life."

A brief span of twenty-one days forcefully brought this home to me. I experienced death and birth and felt deeply connected to both. Ultimately, I realised that life itself truly is eternal. As a direct outcome of this experience, two years later, I was able to make a wonderful trip to Hall of the Great Vow for kosen-rufu, do Gongyo with Sensei and make my own vow "To reveal my Buddhahood, not to be afraid and to show actual proof of the law in my life, exactly where I am".

Neha Budhia's Experience

The Daishonin assures us that no prayer of the votary of the Lotus Sutra goes unanswered and that there is no good karma that does not begin to work on one's behalf.

He says, "It is like the case of the fishing net: though the net is composed of innumerable small meshes, when one pulls the main cord of the net, there are no meshes that do not move. Or it is like a garment: though the garment is composed of countless tiny threads when one pulls on a corner of the garment, there are no threads that aren't drawn along." ('A Sage and an Unenlightened Man', WND – 1)

In the year 2014, I, Neha Budhia, was introduced to this life changing philosophy. I recall the time when I went for lunch with a friend and she just casually spoke about the practice. At once, I was intrigued to know more and get into it at the earliest.

When I was introduced to the practice, I had no idea what I was getting into. I just understood that the philosophy was aimed at spreading happiness for oneself and happiness for others. At that stage of my life I just wanted to meet new people and thought that this was the perfect platform.

I plunged into the practice, not having much meaning attached to it. I started attending meetings and doing daimoku with my seniors in faith. However, I always had an unflinching faith in the practice. I knew this was no coincidence. As years passed, I grew closer to the practice and became even more regular. I was soon appointed the District Cubs Division leader. Years went by, and I kept drifting along. I started noticing the inconspicuous benefits I was receiving through the Mystic Law.

However, it was only in the last one year, in 2018, that I consciously exerted myself towards the practice and the cubs. One fine day, there was something that stirred inside me and I started meeting people who incidentally wanted to know about our philosophy. Mystically, I was able to shakabuku (introduce) 8 people into the practice, last year. That, I guess, was the turning point in my life. However, my life condition still kept wavering, from a complete low life state to an extreme state of happiness. The Daishonin says and I quote "As practice progresses and understanding grows, the three obstacles and four devils emerge in confusing form, vying with one another to interfere. One should neither be influenced nor frightened by them". I knew that I had to take charge of my life and started chanting with vigour and stronger determination.

On the personal front, I have been married for 6 years now and had decided to plan a family in 2016. I increased my practice and started home-visiting people in my district. Subconsciously, I was doing it only out of selfish reasons. Later on, one day while chanting in front of the Gohonzon, I heard an inner voice that told me that kosen-rufu is about dedicating oneself selflessly towards others' victories and happiness. This small shift in my attitude had a great impact.

My life was transforming slowly but surely, when in the month of November 2018, even after trying for a baby for two years, my husband and I decided to go for assisted technology (ivf) for our kosen-rufu baby. Little did I know that my shakabuku friend from London would be coming for two months during that period of my procedure. She completely changed my perspective about the philosophy. My journey of human revolution and internal karmic shift had begun 5 years ago, but as the Gosho states 'winter always turns to spring'.

In December 2018, I was guided to chant immensely for the right kosen-rufu baby to come into our lives. I went in for my first day of IVF with full confidence, knowing and being assured that I was winning. I chanted vigorous daimoku and did more than 2 or 3 home visits daily, alongside my strict work regime. I exerted myself in every way for kosen-rufu and towards encouraging members in front of me, forgetting about my victories. Little did I realize that, the first time was only preparing me for a negative result.

I recall the words of President Ikeda, "Some problems are karmic in nature. Their "roots lie deep in causes made in the past. They are like illnesses that require strong medication, even surgery, and prolonged care. We need to be patient and hopeful while facing such karmic problems." (Discussions on Youth-2)

When the results came, with the power of Nam-myoho-renge-kyo, and remembering the words of our mentor, I was very calm and composed. There was a sense of patience in me. My husband and my family become a bedrock of support. I believed that an integral part of our prayer is the action we take based on faith. It would be wrong to adopt an easy-going attitude, make no efforts to achieve our desired goals and just wait for our prayers to work. Hence, when we went in for a second round of IVF, we surrendered totally to the Gohonzon and the universe. I was rest assured that our kosen-rufu baby would come to us at the right time. I followed the guidance given by my shakabuku friend to chant wholeheartedly for my baby to be 'an agent of change' in this world and 'to give gratitude to the unborn child who was transforming my husband's and my family's karma'.

I exerted myself wholeheartedly in Gakkai activities and home visits. On 16th March 2019, I chanted for 3 hour 20 minutes for the first time, for the victory of the All India Youth Division campaign, being held on 31st March 2019.

On 27th March 2019, I got my result and this time it was positive. On the same day, I was also awarded the Young Achievers Award in the Education category by a prestigious organization in India. I simply could not believe my ears! It was all happening. Finally. The Gohonzon was rewarding me in all directions, at the same time. My prayers had been answered. My family and I were ecstatic. Our happiness knew no bounds. Next week, on 2nd April, we went in for our first early pregnancy scan and were blessed with the news of twins. This was incredible.

Currently, I am in my first trimester. With immense gratitude to the Gohonzon and to all my comrades in faith who helped me on this life transforming journey, I am determined to spread the law and wholeheartedly foster each individual in front of me. To conclude, I would like to quote Daisaku Ikeda from his book 'Flowers of Hope', guidance for the women's division:

"There is no flower without a root, and if it is to bloom, it must be fed by something strong and steady". And it is precisely because the women's division members are devotedly cultivating these invisible yet all important roots that the Soka Gakkai blooms so luxuriously with the flowers of happiness, capable individuals and victory.

Thank you.

Neha Dutt's Experience

My name is Neha Dutt and I've been practicing Nichiren Buddhism for almost 16 years. However, the duration of my practice doesn't really mean anything on its own. It's only when things got difficult, over the last 6 years, that my practice truly deepened. Till then I was happily chugging along, content at relatively minor victories, and at challenging superficial aspects of life. My journey, in short, is about how I learnt what it truly means to stop applying the strategy of my mind, and instead to open up my life to the unfathomably powerful strategy of the Lotus Sutra.

Now what exactly did that mean? I didn't know either at that point. But I intended to find out. I decided to study about it and found this great guidance from Guidelines of Faith by Satoru Izumi:

"When difficulty arises, don't assume a casual attitude, thinking, "Because I've been chanting daimoku, the problem will somehow solve itself." Instead, take the matter seriously, pray to the Gohonzon to change poison into medicine, and courageously challenge your problem. Your earnest prayer will bring forth abundant wisdom and vigorous energy from within, which in turn will enable you to find a way out of your situation, no matter how adverse it may be.

No matter what situation may confront you, don't allow yourself to become completely caught up in means and methods, but put into practice the teaching in the Gosho which states, "Employ the strategy of the Lotus Sutra before any other." Establish an attitude of "Daimoku first under any and all circumstances." Then, based on your daimoku, you can work out the best method. This is the prime point of faith, a posture centred on the Gohonzon.

Human beings are inclined to seek comfort and shun difficulties. Remember, however, that one can only train and improve himself through struggle and effort. Be a person of unswerving faith who chants persistently, no matter what may occur.

When something good happens, regard it as a benefit from the Gohonzon and chant daimoku in heartfelt appreciation. When something bad happens, recognise that the only way to change it fundamentally is through faith in the Gohonzon, and chant daimoku in earnest. If you maintain pure faith in this way for five years, ten years, twenty years and so on, upholding the attitude of "Gohonzon first" and "Daimoku first", your life will naturally follow a course along which all of your desires will be fulfilled."

As I began to put daimoku first, I realized that after trying to conceive naturally for two long years, I couldn't keep doing the same thing and expecting different results. Nichiren Daishonin writes, "If you try to treat someone's illness without knowing its cause, you will only make the person sicker than before." (WND, The Actions of the Votary of the Lotus Sutra).

What was the cause of this illness then? After those first two years of trying, which involved consecutive months of crying in the washroom at work when I found out my periods had started yet again, I decided it was time to investigate what was wrong. I had already developed a fairly large suite of allergies after coming to the UK, due to being over-prescribed antibiotics (three times the maximum dosage for ten days), which tore out my gut lining. My immune system was attacking itself, but I didn't realise at that time the crucial role this played in hindering conception. My husband wasn't practising Buddhism then, but was very supportive of starting all investigations, including for himself.

I have a fairly obsessive personality and in the two years of trying to conceive, I had become obsessed with food as a means to distract myself from the seemingly endless continuum of disappointments. Food became my life and every meal had to be a grand one. My husband and I both sought refuge in food and consequently both put on a lot of weight. In our spare time we watched MasterChef, Man vs Food, Jamie's 30-minute meals, Nigella's Kitchen – if there was a program related to food, we were watching it. It came as no surprise after we got our test results back that I had PCOS (a combination of a stressful, sedentary job and poor diet) and my husband had a slightly low count due to the punishingly long hours at work.

Through this time, though I was practising strongly, and was YWD leader in Docklands then and in Highgate district, I knew I wasn't addressing something fundamental in my life. Instead of using the strategy of the Lotus Sutra, I was busy trying my own strategies every month, wasting vast amounts of money on all kinds of painful treatments and external solutions. Sometimes the longest journey is the one to the Gohonzon. I realised I was chanting for everything and everyone else but somehow couldn't bring myself to chant about this. I didn't want to look at it in the face, as I was afraid of what would show up. And when I did sit down to chant, I realised I was pleading. A reflection of insecurity, fear and lack of belief in my prayer.

I mystically came across this guidance from President Toda on active prayer, "The prayer to the Gohonzon is completely different from that found in a dependent, supplicant faith; we do not weakly and passively beg someone for salvation or assistance. Prayer in Nichiren Buddhism is fundamentally a vow. It is a pledge or commitment to follow a chosen course of action; it is a declaration to challenge a clear objective."

Therein began my journey to chant with a clear objective – to challenge the known and unknown roadblocks that lay between me and my unborn child.

The journey from 2013, when we got married and started trying to conceive, till 2018, when we had our baby boy, has been one of the most arduous ones in my life. I almost didn't make it many times. I chanted deeply about my job and my lifestyle and felt that the long, stressful hours at work were no longer in sync with where my health and my heart were headed. I decided to resign from investment banking at a time when a lot of people were being fired. Everyone thought I was insane to let go of such a prestigious job where I was one of the youngest Vice Presidents at the bank, responsible for the country risk and portfolio management of over 90 countries. I needed some time out to get my health back in order, to reflect about my kosen-rufu job and in the meantime write a book on the life of Indians in London - something I'd always wanted to do.

My husband was very supportive of my decision and though we kept trying to conceive, we were met with disappointment after disappointment. Months became years. At this point I sought guidance as a lot of anger was building up towards this life that refused to come to us.

A beautiful, compassionate YWD leader whom I deeply respect, told me to chant with gratitude towards my unborn child, as this life was already teaching us so much and awakening us in so many ways - making us aware of all the critical lifestyle changes we needed to make etc.

I began chanting gratitude daimoku to this life but at the same time, found that the lifestyle changes we needed to make, required tremendous self-discipline. Given that we had become slaves to our palates, we often slid back in our diets, giving ourselves weekends off and holidays of binging. It came as no surprise that we just couldn't conceive. A family doctor in India recommended getting an HSG done to check whether my Fallopian tubes were blocked. I was determined to leave no stone unturned so despite my fear of medical treatments, I decided to go ahead and get the test done.

The doctor had said to take a painkiller 2 hours before my scheduled appointment time. I did so but due to a massive traffic jam in Delhi, the doctor rocked up 3 hours late. In all the stress, I completely forgot that the painkiller's effect would have worn off and went in for the procedure and felt excruciating pain throughout. I was in agony for 3 days, but the good news was that my tubes were not blocked. Also, the family doctor said not to rule out conceiving within the next three months as often couples conceive after an HSG, which apparently flushes out any minor blockages in the Fallopian tubes.

I had the HSG in January and much to my delight I conceived in February! However, I felt incredibly exhausted all the time and just couldn't stay awake. Then the period cramps started and at 7 weeks I had a miscarriage. I remember going for all the post miscarriage check-ups alone, filled with fear at what was happening to me and upset at the life that had come to us but left so soon. It felt cruel. Life felt cruel. I was in excruciating pain and my suffering knew no bounds. I received great protection though, as no internal procedures needed to be done, which can sometimes leave internal scars. It was a clean miscarriage, they said.

The day after my miscarriage something very interesting happened. I was to host a Buddhist meeting at my place. I texted my WD leader requesting her to cancel it. However, a certain member didn't receive the message in time, and he came over. I didn't have the heart to send him away and to be honest, I was grateful for some company as my husband was coming back late again from work.

I told this member what had happened, wobbling and sniffling throughout. He was incredibly strong, non-judgmental and unfazed (some people get uncomfortable in such situations and don't know what to say or do). He was a real Buddha. We decided to chant for an hour. His daimoku was like thunder. I cannot describe it in words, but somewhere along the hour, something in me shifted. I felt a deep-rooted strength rear its majestic head. In that moment, I re-determined. I found, in what I thought was a broken me, a renewed strength to challenge the situation. I kept Sensei's words about the transience of life close to heart "Right now your life may be filled with suffering. But just as pleasure never lasts forever, neither does suffering."

Soon after my miscarriage, I got back to attending Buddhist meetings regularly and signed up for a year of dedicated lilac at the London Ikeda Peace Centre (LIPC). I often went twice or thrice a month to lilac, thinking, wishing and chanting that the next time I came, surely, I would be pregnant – I was doing so many activities after all! But again, months became years.

I ended up doing two years of dedicated lilac at LIPC. The smile I forced myself to wear while 'lilacing' became more and more difficult to hold. Often, I would feel my eyes well-up with frustration and anger, but I completed the activity and encouraged every person I met, greeting them with as genuine a smile as I could muster, remembering to shine as a disciple Sensei would be proud of. And after each such activity, I felt another brick in the wall of strength being laid within me.

One evening when I was 'lilacing', I recognised a Women's Division member who had shared an experience about having a second child and the difficult karma she had transformed in doing so. I went to her during my break and broke down. The flood gates of frustration couldn't hold up anymore. She heard me patiently and said, "Look, don't lie to yourself. If you feel having this baby is impossible, chant to make the impossible possible! That's what our practice is about!"

I began to do just that going forward. As a result, a lot of limitations that I had planted within myself bubbled up to the surface, for me to transform. It was like a process of successive approximation – gradually bringing me closer to the truth and giving me bite-sized, tailor-made chunks of karma to transform at each stage, according to the time and capacity. I also got all the right guidance and nudges I needed along the way. For example, at a discussion meeting in Highgate, a 93 year old men's division member, who rarely spoke, said something that really stayed with me. He said (I'm paraphrasing) "We're constantly asking for our prayers to be answered. But if we're practising Nichiren Buddhism correctly, we should be asking ourselves what we need to change within us, to be ready to receive what we want."

I realised that I had never asked myself that question. As I began chanting about it, I realised that I was constantly strategising with my mind. I couldn't somehow bring myself to apply the strategy of the Lotus Sutra - I reminded myself what that meant and began to chant to release the fear of relinquishing control. From the time I identified this to the point where I was able to change it, took over two years.

I had a lot of actual proof along the way - I was able to find my kosen-rufu job in environment finance, where I joined as an intern but was promoted three times within the span of two years, to senior policy advisor. I was able to write and self-publish my book despite struggling with serious bouts of wanting to give up along the way. I successfully completed a course on Sustainability Leadership from

Cambridge University and got a distinction. And most importantly, I was able to deepen my relationship with my husband.

I also deepened my Buddhist study and began to read the Art of Living cover to cover and really digest what was written there. I often had questions in faith, but I had the good fortune of taking them to people who could give me the right answers which propelled to deepen my faith even further. For example, I really loved the fact that in this practice, there was nothing you couldn't chant for and that earthly desires were enlightenment. I loved that because – let's face it – I had a long shopping list of earthly desires. And *numero uno* on that list was having a baby.

My question was – although attachments and desires can cause unhappiness, if in Buddhism we believe that earthly desires are enlightenment and if one is encouraged to chant to fully manifest one's desires, can't it make one obsessive and intensify the suffering? Given that I already had an obsessive personality, chanting so fervently to have a baby was akin to pouring fuel on the fire, and all I was thinking of all day, every second of the day was baby, baby, baby!

I went for guidance to a leader in East Finchley. She smoked, had a raspy voice, a wicked laugh and a fair few bottles of Absolut in her studio apartment. Aha! Earthly desires can indeed lead to enlightenment, I thought, reassured. When she heard my story, about how I was obsessing and how I wanted to reconcile that in the realm of faith, she very succinctly said, "You can have all the earthly desires you want, just don't suffer them. If your desire becomes an obsession, it causes suffering. Learn from that and transform that." That brought me one step closer. I began to chant with that added focus and began to learn to still enjoy life despite being childless. I came across this great study in the Heart of the Lotus Sutra (pg. 68-70: The wisdom to discern the true nature of attachments):

"The fundamental cause of people's unhappiness lies in their tendency to develop attachments of various kinds. An attachment, just as it sounds, is a fetter on one's heart; it indicates earthly desires, cravings and the like.

The spirit of the Lotus Sutra, however, is not to eradicate earthly desires. When we base ourselves on the Mystic Law, we can transform desires – just as they are – into enlightenment. This is the principle of earthly desires are enlightenment.

The truth is that we could not in fact eradicate are attachments even if we so wished. For the sake of argument, even if it was feasible, doing so would make it impossible to live in the real world. What is important is that we make full use of our attachments rather than allowing them to control us. In order to do that, it is necessary that we clearly recognise them for what they are."

President Toda also urges us to make full use of our attachments:

"The Gohonzon enables us to perceive our attachments just as they are. Because we have attachments, we can lead interesting and significant lives. Our faith enables us to maintain these attachments in such a way that they do not cause us suffering. Rather than being controlled by our attachments, we need to fully use our attachments to become happy."

In short, we should cause the firewood of earthly desires to burn high and, to that same extent, chant Nam-myoho-renge-kyo sincerely and take action. In doing so, our earthly desires become a springboard to propel us toward our attainment of Buddhahood.

When we clearly establish a fundamental objective in life, we can use our attachments most fully and profitably. We can turn them into tailwinds to propel us toward happiness.

After a few months passed, my mind started strategising again and I felt the panic of the proverbial "clock ticking." It had been a rough month and I had hosted two baby showers. The pretence and hypocrisy of happiness was getting to me. Why was everyone else so fortunate? I knew I shouldn't compare and that it didn't change a thing, but sometimes it was but natural to feel singled out. I kept this guidance from Daisaku Ikeda close to my heart:

"Fortunate circumstances don't guarantee happiness, and, conversely, hard circumstances don't guarantee that one will be unhappy.

Our environment doesn't decide our happiness; we do. We are either defeated by our environment or we triumph over it. That's what determines our happiness.

There are many troubling, painful, unpleasant, and worrisome things in life. When you face such things, you have two options. You can complain, blame the environment, and be defeated. Some may express sympathy for you, but, ultimately, you're the one to lose out, and anything you say will really be just an excuse. The second option is to live with an invincible spirit, blazing your own way regardless of your environment. The choice is up to you."

We decided to try IUI. From a medical perspective, everything was perfect. I remember being in an extremely elevated life condition when going in for the final procedure, and feeling thrilled when the doctor informed me that there was a high chance I'd have twins. During the two-week wait that followed, I amped up my activities, study and chanting, but sadly I felt the same old cramps and sure enough, my periods started soon after. I was devastated.

The day my periods started, I received a frantic phone call from a YWD I used to support in a previous district. She said she just had to see me. I was in no position or frame of mind to see anyone but something in me agreed to see her. When she came over, she announced she was pregnant. I felt my heart plummet to the floor. What cruel trick was the universe playing again with me, I wondered? However, I kept a smiling face and congratulated her. But she broke down and said there was no need to congratulate as she was planning to terminate the pregnancy as she'd discovered that her baby had several defects which would mean that even if she would be born, there was a high chance she would suffer a lot and not live very long. This girl was torn about terminating the pregnancy and was ridden with guilt about taking the decision to terminate this life inside her.

As we chanted it really hit me that getting pregnant didn't necessarily equal being happy. And when I looked around at my friends who were parents, apparently neither did being a parent equal being happy. As we chanted for the unborn life inside this member to fulfil her mission, I realised the deep strength one needed to be a mother, especially to a kosen-rufu child, who comes with a great mission.

However, having our baby still eluded us. At the time, I was going for a fairly painful form of non-TCM acupuncture, where they twist needles in until you feel in electric current surge through your veins. I remember all the sessions and all the times I screamed out in pain. I remember rushing from work thrice a week to this clinic, only to come back tired, sore and feeling like I didn't want to live any more. There was just no fun left in life anymore. However, suicide seemed like too much of an effort as well. I was completely flat lining inside.

At a study meeting in Muswell Hill, Kazuo Fuji said, "Look, it's already the month of July. When we look at the seven months of the year gone by, can we honestly say we've made all out efforts in faith? If not, wouldn't *now* be a good time to do so? When we look back at this year, we should know with relief and gratitude that we've been able to carve out great victories in our lives and shift fundamental karma!"

That spoke to me and I really took that on. I held a ten-hour tozo in August 2017. I felt a deep expansion of my life state after that but the next month still nothing happened. Frustrated, I resorted to strategising with my mind and decided to sign up for IVF with the NHS. Somehow the speed at which things progressed for me was unheard of, especially at Guys and St. Thomas' Hospital, where I was to have my procedure. The funding got approved within a month! I decided to go in for the procedure on 8th November 2018. However, everything in my mind and body screamed out "NO!" for IVF.

Given all that was wrong with my body, the hormone imbalance, the PCOS, the immune system attacking itself etc, putting myself through all the various hormones and injections required for IVF felt wrong at every level. The more I chanted about it, the more crystal clear it became that my body wasn't ready for it. However, my husband and I had already been through so much that I didn't want to leave any stone unturned anymore and I was really running out of patience. I signed up for Chinese acupuncture on the advice of a leader, who said this particular practitioner had helped a lot of women conceive. The woman, probably a mirror of my low life state, injured two veins in my wrist by putting needles in and adding electrodes with too high a voltage and I was in severe pain. I told her off and she said she wouldn't treat me anymore as I wasn't complying and as I couldn't take even a little pain! I was in agony – mentally and physically. But, despite blue-green bruised veins and tingling fingers, I decided not to give up. I apologised and kept going to her.

During the month of September, we had a setback – my husband had left his job without any options to hand. And I had my first panic attack. I didn't know I was having a panic attack then and I thought I was going to die, as I just couldn't breathe, and my chest felt like it had seized up. It wasn't pleasant, as I'm sure anyone who's had one can attest to. Mystically, again, I received great protection. When the ambulance came, there was an old paramedic who had been posted in Afghanistan during the war. He took my husband aside and told him what was happening to me...a panic attack. He held my hand and in the most reassuring way ever, just kept talking to me calmly, asking me to breathe, showing me that all my vital signs were normal, cracking jokes about his stints with cooking Indian food etc. He waited with me till I had calmed down.

Shortly after the panic attack, one day at work, I booked myself a meeting room and broke down sobbing uncontrollably. I was horribly lost and didn't know what to do next. I really didn't want to live anymore. I was truly fed up of life - I had endured too much pain in my opinion, and so much pain lay ahead of me. There was nothing to look forward to and since we had unexplained infertility, I didn't even know where to aim the arrow of my daimoku. Also, I had completely lost interest in eating and I dropped 15 kilograms in the span of two months. Friends we met asked if I was alright, given I looked so sickly, and this made me retreat even more. I began going through some guidance on my phone and came across two bits of guidance that boosted my flailing spirits:

1.   Sensei: "Young people who face daunting challenges but fight vigorously to overcome them go on to become far more capable and resilient than those who lead lives of ease and comfort. They will achieve far greater things than those whose lives are always smooth sailing."

2.   Danny Nagashima (extract from his article on becoming people of unlimited self-esteem), "Your mission as a Buddhist is to become happy – not to master suffering."

I realised that I had indeed become a black belt at suffering. I also realised that I had to stop suffering alone. I needed to talk to a professional about what was happening within me – there was a chasm between my conscious and unconscious mind that I was unable to bridge.

I decided to contact a distant family friend who had apparently become a well-respected hypnotherapist and counsellor in London. I'd never spoken to him on a personal level before, but after listening to how broken I was, he agreed to see me fairly quickly (normally, he has a wait list of over a month).

Through some extremely productive sessions with him, I was able to identify that I had a paralysing fear of hospitals and a terrifying "hospitals equal death" belief due to the several years that my father (my best friend) had suffered from an auto-immune progressive disease and eventually passed away in hospital. Through regression sessions, I learnt that one of my earliest memories was lighting a candle in the dark, tears streaming down my face as I prayed deeply to God to give me all the afflictions and pain that riddled my father's body. It pained me so deeply to see his face contorted in pain so often, although he was a titan of strength – never complaining, never giving into self-pity or despair. But somewhere along the 19 long years that my father suffered, I had developed a very deep-rooted subconscious belief that I didn't deserve to be healthy or happy. And that began manifesting at a conscious level in my mind and body.

My therapist told me several sessions later when I was more stable, that I had acute Post Traumatic Stress Disorder (PTSD) and that my sympathetic brain was spotting danger everywhere – he gave the analogy of a gazelle only running when it was being chased by a lion (external trigger), but in my case my gazelle (my flight or fight hormone/sympathetic brain) was constantly on the run! It found no solace or security in anything. It was no wonder then that my body couldn't support another life.

We did some empowering practices of "healing the inner child" together. I learnt to have faith and give more muscle to developing the "capable adult" in me. I also learnt not to scold or chide the child in me, when she fearfully ran to me for comfort. Or not to hate my body when my immune system attacked itself yet again. Acceptance was a very difficult but a very key lesson.

I saw so clearly, that I first had to learn to be a mother to myself, before I could even think of introducing another life.

The sessions with my therapist were painful – "house cleaning isn't easy" as he says, "Dirt comes out." I had to relive and find cathartic exits out of various traumatic instances in my life, where I had suppressed screams. I was shaken but slowly getting stronger. I was also moving a few steps closer towards mastering my mind.

As Daisaku Ikeda writes, "While controlling your mind, which is at once both extremely subtle and solemnly profound, you should strive to elevate your faith with freshness and vigour. When you do so, both your life and your surroundings will open wide before you and every action you take will become a source of benefit. Understanding the subtle workings of one's mind is the key to faith and attaining Buddhahood in this lifetime."

In parallel, I also signed up for yoga at a place called Yoga in Daily Life in Queens Park. One of the best decisions I have ever made. The main yogic guru from Rajasthan had come one weekend to London to give a lecture. I was only able to make it for the last ten minutes of the lecture. His words hit me like a lightning bolt. He could have spoken about any topic under the sun, but he chose to speak about life. And he said, "This planet doesn't need more people. We have already burdened it with too many of us. If we are thinking of introducing more lives to this world, please ensure that they are strong and generous and that that they add love, laughter and light to the world. And for that, we need to first be humans who have such qualities in us, so that we can enshrine such qualities in them."

That details of that day are etched in my memory with crystal clearness. It was a truly epiphanic moment for me. I found renewed focus in my prayers. Along with chanting to heal and accept my body and the inner child in me, and become a capable adult, I also began chanting to become a mother who would enable the life she attracted to bring love, laughter and light to the world.

My mother meanwhile had decided to come to London to be with me for the first two weeks of my IVF treatment. She landed on 7th November, and I remember taking a pregnancy test at Heathrow Airport and much to my utter amazement, it was positive!

I waited till I got home and re-took the test and it was positive again! My mother had done a one million daimoku campaign for me to get pregnant naturally. All our prayers manifested. I remember wondering what to do the next day when I was scheduled to start the IVF procedure, given that it was still very early days of my pregnancy and given that I had had a miscarriage in the past.

I called the hospital. The lady I spoke to, very kindly said that the funding would still be available for the rest of the financial year but hopefully, she said, she'd never hear from me again!

I had an extremely painful and sickly pregnancy with very low blood pressure, nausea and severe weakness and terrible, terrifying, often crippling levels of anxiety. I still wasn't eating much. My husband still didn't have a job then and I remember stressing about our fast-depleting levels of finances. I would wake up at 3am every morning, ridden with a fear of the unknown, of how and when things would fall into place. How would we manage our expenses, how would we bring up our child? I didn't want my child to come into a world of lack and limitation. So, I stopped giving energy to that feeling and I decided to challenge the fear.

Every day, without fail, when my eyes fell open at 3am, I chanted for an hour and did a deep yogic breathing meditation which calmed me down and really sustained me through my pregnancy. I was also very fortunate to have an extremely supportive boss, whose kindness, understanding and support throughout my pregnancy made me deepen my belief that the protective functions in my universe were in action.

I could see that the protective functions, or shoten zenjin, were really activated in my environment. I had to trust that they would continue to be so, and that through strong faith, everything else would also fall into place. My husband, who was chanting regularly at this point and attending meetings, was praying for his kosen-rufu job.

We invested in a course he wanted to pursue in Social Finance from Oxford University, which was a considerable amount from our savings. I knew I had to support him to become happy and to achieve his full potential. He enjoyed the course and made a lot of connections there and set up his own company, advising socially impactful companies on raising investment capital. But there still wasn't a steady stream of income.

As my pregnancy progressed, I developed gestational diabetes and as the delivery date came near, the doctors explained they'd need to intervene as they couldn't let the pregnancy go to term, due to risks of still birth associated with gestational diabetes.

Again, I knew my body couldn't take all the hormone injections etc, so I chanted deeply for protection. I was also given guidance to set a date for delivery linked with kosen-rufu.

I was to be induced on 11th June with injections, but I explained to my doctor that I really wanted it to happen naturally. She was most considerate and said they could try a swab test which could possibly trigger natural labour pain. It did!

I chanted to have my baby on 6th June, Tsunesaburo Makiguchi's birthday. My son was born on that very day. I had the most amazing, compassionate midwives anyone could have prayed for, who made me feel well-looked after and kept us laughing with their amazing sense of humour.

After two days of contractions, when the actual pushing began, my son was out in half an hour. He entered this world to the sound of Nam-myoho-renge-kyo (which I had playing on loop) and giggles, as the mid-wife asked my husband, "Are you sure you're the father? I can see a blond head coming out!"

I had the most uncomplicated labour, with no antibiotics or hormone injections, no tears or grazes.

The gratitude I feel for this practice, this organisation, our mentors and all the incredible members who supported me cannot be expressed in words. And last but not the least - another victory – my husband got a job in his desired field of impact investing in May, a month before I gave birth. When our son joined us, he came into a world of love, laughter, light and abundance, just as I had prayed for.

When I look back at all the protection I received, I am speechless. The palatable and the unpalatable phases, both brought with them great lessons. All the suffering I underwent introduced me to my Buddhahood, to surprising levels of strength and resilience that resided in me, unknown to me. My journey enabled me to meet incredible people, forge lifelong, powerful friendships and deepen existing relationships, showing me all the while that all poison can be turned into medicine.

The painful acupuncture showed me that I could indeed handle a lot of pain, without medication. The past trauma in my life that bubbled up to the surface, allowed me to heal it. I got the inner wisdom and strength to change my diet and align my body to food right for my constitution instead of being a slave to my palate. My immune system gradually began to heal and stop attacking itself and most importantly, I spiritually healed myself (disease first manifests itself at the spiritual level and then at the physical level as per Buddhist study).

The angels who supported me whenever I seemed to reach an impasse in faith – my therapist Shomit, my yoga teachers, my current boss, my husband, my mother, my SGI family in London (especially Pji and Sylvie), all the leaders and members who encouraged me – all emerged to bring me to this day when I, an evolving mother to myself and my son, am able to write this experience, overwhelmed with oceans of gratitude. We have been able to carve out 360 degree, 'surround-sound' victories in our lives.

I vowed when our son was born, to collate a book of experiences on starting families. I would have loved to read such a book when I was going through what I was, unable to talk about it to anyone, suffering alone and feeling deepening levels of despair with our diagnosis of "unexplained infertility."

No one should have to go through that alone anymore – and no one should feel ashamed to talk about it. Although everyone's situation is unique, all seemingly obstinate karma can be changed if we equip ourselves with the tools of Nichiren Buddhism and learn what it means to apply the strategy of the Lotus Sutra.

Also, I've learnt that there's no such thing as a coincidence in the realm of faith – the district that I moved to after our son was born, had two YWDs who were struggling to get pregnant. When I went on maternity leave to India, the girl I introduced to the practice was struggling with conception issues and I was able to support her through a failed IVF. She is now expecting twins and has shared her experience in this book.

I want to dedicate my life to empowering people through this faith and manifesting the vision for worldwide kosen-rufu. I know that challenges will keep coming but I am confident that I will transform them with the tools of faith that I have found in this practice. I feel I am no longer hostage to my self-imposed limitations. Rather, I am a willing host to a life-long celebration to explore the boundless potential of being human. I want to live life full-stride, with courage, compassion, confidence and joy brimming in my heart - we are not born to master suffering.

I would like to end with a quote from Sensei,

"There is a place inside me that has never given up. I chant focusing on it. I appreciate it and let Buddhahood become the strongest force in my life. My passion for kosen-rufu must become like a volcanic eruption. Every vein, every cell of my body must exude Buddhahood. My face must glow and eyes sparkle like a Buddha. I am a person of unlimited self-esteem, unlimited mental, physical, emotional resources and health. Let daimoku reach my fundamental darkness - ignorance, illusion, doubt, fear, anxiety and sickness. I will fight like a lion, no matter what. I am born to win. And I will win, win, win!"

Robyn's Experience

For several years now, one of my biggest struggles has been with anxiety, first triggered by losing 3 friends to suicide. Through the last decade, 10 significant people have passed away and after each one I experienced 6 months of debilitating anxiety. Through challenging this karma, it has transformed from something I was deeply ashamed of, to something I use to encourage others.

When my husband and I found out we were pregnant, we were thrilled. As we got closer to our first scan, anxiety began to emerge, and I became plagued by the fear that we had had a missed miscarriage. To our relief, the scan showed our baby was healthy and progressing well.

18 weeks into my pregnancy, my anxiety returned and one morning I began to have intrusive thoughts about suicide. I didn't have a desire to act on them, but the thoughts were persistent, overwhelming and terrifying. Whenever I have faced illness, I have chanted to receive the best possible medical care. This manifested in being able to make 5 phone calls that day, in the midst of the struggle, to reach out for help. By the evening, I had a support plan in place, though the thoughts had become intrusive visions of my own funeral which I found deeply distressing.

I phoned a senior leader for guidance about how to best use faith activities to transform this karma. My tendency in the past was to say yes to every opportunity to support an SGI activity and I have never regretted it. Time and time again, I have experienced the power of using activities to transform my life. However, at this point in my pregnancy, I felt that it was important not to over extend myself, but I struggled with old familiar karma - the idea that what I was offering was never enough, the efforts I was making weren't enough, that I am not enough.

She encouraged me to say yes to any activity that filled me with joy and no to everything else at this time and to prioritise taking great care of my health. I had two responsibilities for our upcoming summer course. I withdrew from one and joyfully poured my life into the other.

I had been on the waiting list for psychotherapy for anxiety and bereavement trauma for over a year. I chanted to get whatever support my life needed and rang the organisation, explaining my increasingly pressing need. Within 2 weeks, my therapy began, and I was also seen by the perinatal mental health team.

My husband and I created our ideal birth plan and I began chanting for an unmedicated water birth at home. Through my daimoku, I began to see that though I felt safe with the idea of our planned labour, I was terrified of what would happen if complications arose. I had a deep fear that a hospital transfer would trigger my anxiety, which in turn would halt labour, causing me to panic, putting myself and my baby at risk. I only trusted my body could do this if my mind stayed out of the way.

I changed my prayer and though I left my birth vision by the Gohonzon, I expanded my prayer and chanted for the safest, happiest birth for our family and for kosen-rufu.

I spoke to a Buddhist friend whose birth plan had been very similar to mine but had ended up being transferred to hospital and having an emergency c-section. She shared that she felt deeply empowered by her experience and the incredible support from the medical team. Inspired by her, I chanted about and wrote down my preferences for any eventuality that might occur during labour. Each day I read – often out loud – the two Goshos 'Easy Delivery of a Fortune Child' and 'The Birth of Tsukimaro.'

One evening, 36 weeks into our pregnancy, I started to have contractions. I rang my midwife and asked what we should do. She said the choice was ours - we could stay at home and the homebirth team would come or we could go to hospital. As the baby was still premature, she explained why her recommendation would be the latter. My husband and I reached the decision that if labour had in fact begun, we would go to hospital in the morning. I felt at peace with this and even a little excited.

When we awoke, the contractions had stopped, but I could see that I had changed. I felt happy and confident with any scenario as long as we were all safe. I reflected on what had helped make the shift and in part it was our midwife's confidence in us as parents to make the best decision. With no outside pressure or agenda, we had the space to check in with our Buddhahood and instincts to choose what felt right for us. So often, I don't take the time to check in with my instincts and end up feeling resentful and bulldozed by other people's opinions. In that moment, I saw how crucial it will be to base our parenting decisions on prayer to the Gohonzon, instead of looking for the 'right' answer from somewhere outside.

When I was 40 weeks and 2 days my labour began and the following morning our daughter was born at home in a birth pool in front of our Gohonzon. We were calm, safe and well, everything had gone exactly as we had hoped for. I was left with an incredible feeling of gratitude and the sense that rather than meeting her for the first time, the three of us had found each other once again.

This first month of getting to know each other has been the happiest of my life and also fantastic training in faith as we challenge exhaustion and our new role as parents. I am continuing my therapy which is helping me understand and manage the vulnerability of loving her so overwhelmingly, of not being able to control everything, of having to deeply trust my life.

We wrote to Sensei to share the news of her birth and our determination to be the kind of parents who can raise a joyous, powerful Bodhisattva of the Earth.

"If the water of your faith is clear, the moon of blessings will surely cast its reflection on it and protect you. You are assured of an easy delivery. A passage from the Lotus Sutra says, "A wonderful Law such as this..." and another says, "She will be delivered safely of a healthy child." From Easy Delivery of a Fortune Child. (pg. 186 of Gosho Vol 1)

Rohan's Experience

I never really thought of what it would be like to be a father, but I always assumed that it would happen at some point. Now – almost one year into fatherhood - I can unreservedly say that although my journey to this point has been punctuated with challenges of various stripes, I know that it has provided me with opportunities to address important aspects of my life. And thankfully, the practice and the support of many (immeasurably wise) SGI members are the reasons that I'm able to hear my son's inexplicably happy and loud gurgles at the break of dawn!

It was a relatively long journey to this point both for me and my wife, who described her experience earlier in this book[1]. We experienced this journey together, but – as anyone who has taken a journey in the London Underground can attest – perspectives of the same journey taken by two people can be quite different.

In retrospect, the challenges I faced were the right ones to polish specific aspects of my life. This belief is captured in the following quote by Daisaku Ikeda, which really inspired me over the last few years:

"Whether we regard difficulties in life as misfortunes or whether we view them as good fortune depends entirely on how much we have forged our inner determination. It all depends on our attitude, our inner state of life. With a dauntless spirit, we can lead a cheerful and thoroughly enjoyable life. We can develop a self of such fortitude that we look forward to life's trials and tribulations with a sense of profound elation and joy: "Come on obstacles! I've been expecting you! This is the chance that I've been waiting for!""

Therefore, I'm grateful for the obstacles I have faced in this journey – from when our son was a mere twinkle in our eyes to now a little human alarm clock – and I've summarised them in the following pages.

---

[1] *See Neha Dutt's experience.*

Ego vs. Health

When Neha and I first realised that conceiving our baby was taking more time that we had envisaged, we discussed seeking medical advice. The doctors eventually asked us to get a suite of tests done. But even though my test was relatively easy to do, I felt this irrational sense of my masculinity being questioned. But on chanting about it over a few days, I realised that it was just my ego making me resist going ahead with the test. I also concluded that any benefits this step might bring could significantly outweigh any reason why I might not want to do it. So, I went ahead.

When the doctors communicated the test results, they advised us that our fertility indicators were borderline and could be sorted out by making lifestyle changes. My life at that time - of working long hours, indulging in decadent food and often punctuating weekends with free-flowing alcohol - was a recipe for personal health disaster. So, I took the doctors' advice on board and over time, I have made those changes (although it still is a continuing challenge).

This obstacle gave me the opportunity to focus on improving my health and provided me with an incentive to make these changes. The wisdom from chanting really helped me to understand my irrational fears and the opportunity to maintain my determination when making extensive life-style changes.

Deafening internal dialogue

I'm wired as a very analytical, solution-focused and positive person (yes, I do realise this sounds like the first line of a cheesy CV). Whilst these characteristics ordinarily hold me in good stead, they have been sorely tested over the last few years.

After Neha had the first miscarriage, my mind went into a tailspin thinking through various scenarios of what could be done, what the benefits and risks of each option were and trying desperately to conclude on the optimal approach. I would go through a similar process every time there was a challenge: when doctors would provide their advice on the next step, when Neha would get a negative in her pregnancy test and at many other times. I often found myself descending into a fog of arguing with myself in my own mind – whilst putting up a significantly calmer façade for Neha's benefit.

The guidance I got was to "take the problem first to the Gohonzon". Although that made sense to me, I found it incredibly hard to not go down the rabbit hole created by my mind. But every time I did take it to the Gohonzon, I felt the fog in my mind lift and I was able to trust more in the strategy of the Lotus Sutra. Although I still struggle with instinctively going to the Gohonzon when I face a challenge, I now place less pressure on my mind to find a solution at every turn. And that is an immensely liberating feeling.

Two to tango

At an SGI Study Meeting, a fellow member had once quoted Daisaku Ikeda:

"Just as a song is a marriage of music and lyrics, husband and wife are equal individuals who, at the same time, perform a single melody of life together. What is important, I think, is how beautiful a song these two life partners can create together."

This does indeed sound beautiful. But a few times – especially in trying circumstances – this beautiful melody can morph into mild cacophony. With monthly dejections, painful therapies and two miscarriages, I realised that the emotional toll that Neha was bearing was getting heavier over time. Consequently, I felt a constant need to support her emotionally. While I was able to provide this (I think) most of the time, sometimes I felt truly at a loss for tools I could use to 'solve the situation'. This would either result in me embittered (unfairly) with Neha's reactions – or Neha feeling that I wasn't able to connect with her emotionally.

When this started happening more frequently – and I was at a loss for tools more often – I realised over time (and evidently the hard way) that while emotional support is important, my goal isn't necessarily for to 'solve the situation' for Neha.

However, deciding to sit down and chant right away was infinitely more powerful than me immediately saying to Neha that "We should speak to another doctor/ therapist" or "It'll happen next time". I chanted not for the solution itself but for me to connect with my own Buddhahood, deeply empathise with what Neha was going through and find the right words to convey my thoughts to her. The second aspect for me was important because (a) empathy is not an attribute that comes naturally to me and (b) as a man, it was immensely difficult to comprehend what Neha was going through. To be honest, it took a lot of effort and patience to do this – and I probably didn't do it as often as I could have. But when I did, the melody did return!

My moon-shot

One of my biggest challenges during this period was when I left my lucrative job at a large investment firm in June 2017. After more than 10 years of working long days and nights in challenging work environments, I wanted to explore a new career in the relatively niche area of impact investing. With the aim of investing capital in solving our world's social and environmental issues, I believed this industry aligned with my own personal values. To get to know this space, I set up my own (one-man) advisory firm, networked extensively and even attended an executive programme at Oxford University in this field – so that I would eventually find the right job in the industry for me. I felt excited about work after a long time and also found that I had headroom to explore aspects of my life that I'd focused less on (health, family, SGI activities and spirituality).

As the Buddhist allegory goes: "One must pull the bow back to make the arrow go further" (partial pun intended). In October 2017, Neha and I realised the fantastic news that we were having a baby! It was what we had wanted for many years and we were ecstatic.

However, the new reality was that I was still finding my footing in a new industry and I didn't have the economic bandwidth my previous jobs afforded. Thankfully we had enough reserves and I had complete faith in myself that I would find the job in my desired field with the three kinds of value, as described by Mr. Makiguchi: Beauty, Benefit and Good. But that was my perspective as a pragmatic optimist.

But as a husband with a pregnant wife, my priorities were different. This uncertainty exacerbated the anxiety Neha experienced. I was incredibly aware of this and I really struggled with supporting her emotionally during the time. I chanted a lot for a solution to this challenge and for the ability to connect with Neha. We also held a full-day Tozo at our house to supercharge our faith. I did more Soka activities and took on more SGI responsibilities. I interviewed with a few firms of my choice, but they were all taking longer than expected in their processes. I also visited my (and Neha's) therapist a few times for guidance on how to emotionally support Neha.

Despite the causes I was putting in, nothing seemed to be moving swiftly enough. However, this also meant that I was able to spend more time with Neha and planning for our baby's imminent arrival. I went with Neha for each of her doctor's examinations – which might not have happened if I was working in my prior job. I also had the bandwidth to meticulously plan the logistics for Neha's delivery.

And then, in March 2018, I got offers from multiple roles at the same time. I chose the one which most closely aligned to my desire to find a job with beauty, benefit and good within impact investing. I started my new role in May 2018, a week after I took Neha on a short holiday on the Scottish coast and a month before our baby was expected. Till then, I'd spent eight months of Neha's pregnancy.

In retrospect, it all worked out beautifully. But when one is in the midst of a challenge, it is difficult to retain that sense of optimism. As Daisaku Ikeda so beautifully states:

"Take heart, and do not let disappointment stop you from moving forward. The true outcome of life is only apparent at the very end."

Happy birthday

Despite the best efforts of our NCT classes and our hypnotherapy coach (neither of which I knew existed as concepts till 6 months previously), I felt woefully unprepared as our baby's 'birth' day approached. There seemed to be so many variables and so many things up in the air. But my role – as a supporting actor in this production – was to confidently plan the logistics and maintain an air of calmness, as I supported Neha through the final stages of giving birth. I trusted that chanting with deep determination to the Gohonzon would make all of this happen.

But although I felt unprepared in my head, my heart believed it would go smoothly. Maybe it was all that chanting (and a hint of exhaustion), but I felt a sense of complete confidence in every action – as though I was on autopilot getting things done. Some of the things were expected: organising a taxi from home to the hospital, badgering nurses for Neha to be seen, calming Neha down (while risking the future usability of my hand in the process). Other things were less expected: booking a hotel room close to the hospital for Neha could stay in till her hospital room got ready. And evidently, my heart was right – I just needed to ignore the doubts in my head and trust myself whole heartedly.

On 6 June 2018 in the morning, aided by two fantastic mid-wives, Neha gave birth to our son. As I held him in my arms, I felt a massive sense of joy (and relief that it all had gone relatively smoothly). I was so proud of Neha – not just for going through labour, but also for the journey she had taken and the obstacles she has overcome.

I've learned more about myself at every step along this journey. The practice has enabled me to actively introspect and provided solutions to the obstacles. Instead of asking "Why me, why now?", I now have the courage to say, "It's better to polish that aspect right now, than carry it around across life-times". The former question is now only reserved for when my son wakes me up at the crack of dawn!

Ruma's Experience

(The contents of this experience have been left completely unchanged and unedited in line with the contributor's wishes).

I would like to start with one of my favourite Nichiren Buddhism quotes - "Suffer what there is to suffer, enjoy what there is to enjoy. Regard both suffering and joy as facts of life and continue chanting Nam-myoho-renge-kyo, no matter what happens. How could this be anything other than the boundless joy of the Law? Strengthen your power of faith more than ever "[WND-1, 681].

My name is Ruma. I am blessed with a loving husband and two beautiful young children. This is the story of my journey of pregnancy, childbirth, motherhood, life of a parent and raising children and how this profound practice of Nichiren Buddhism enabled me to be an extremely capable, courageous & empowered woman to take on the challenges of life with joy.

Few lines about the philosophy of Buddhism - The philosophy of this Buddhist practice itself is so very intriguing i.e. cause and effect. Buddhism teaches that everything in the universe embodies the law of cause & effect. The purpose of Buddhist practice is to transform our basic life tendency or karma by chanting Nam-myoho-renge-kyo, in order to realize our total human potential in this lifetime and beyond. When we chant Nam-myoho-renge-kyo, we tap into the deepest level of consciousness, the pure Buddha nature that is free from all karmic impediments, and thus we are empowered to face our destiny and change it. We create our own present and future by the choices we make in each moment. Understood in this light, the law of cause & effect empowers us, as our every action can serve as a cause that will contribute to creating a better world, both for ourselves and for all around us [https://www.sgi.org/resources/introductory-materials/cause-and-effect.html].

I started practising Nichiren Buddhism in December 2010. At the time, I was just a new practitioner trying to get to know this amazing practice and little did I know in those moments about what a profound journey I was in for! I didn't have the GOHONZON at the time. I had just moved to the UK from India with my partner. I had a decent paying job in the city. As I had just started practising, I would say I was a believer, not really a practitioner. I started gradually with initially attending a few meetings however what I really enjoyed was chatting and meeting new people through the practice. The experiences of the members which were shared in the discussion meetings were so inspiring, invigorating, sometimes spine-chilling and so unbelievable that an outsider would wonder if they were actually achievable.

I was enjoying reading about Nichiren Buddhism too, the Gosho excerpts and the Words of Wisdom, the Art of Living magazine which is our monthly magazine, all of these little gems seemed to be jewels of an everlasting crown of joy and happiness. I started to gradually enjoy chanting Nam-myoho-renge-kyo. In few months I found myself deeply immersed in chanting, studying more about Nichiren Buddhism and engaging with activities across my district and overall SGI as well.

At this point in our lives, we were happily enjoying just being with each other and travelling together to new destinations. As a couple we had sort of decided that we won't have a child until we truly felt like becoming parents, only when we are ready to take on the responsibility of a child, we would go for it. From time to time our parents would put subtle pressure on us to have a child sooner than later which we always politely ignored.

At the end of 2011, we decided that now was the right time and we also felt ready as a couple to start a family, hence we decided we are going to have a baby in 2012. I was lucky to get pregnant exactly when I wanted to. It was like a dream come true. My pregnancy was confirmed in April 2012. We both were just ecstatic and very happy, just delighted to imagine that soon we will become parents and were eagerly looking forward to our baby. We decided we would wait until the first trimester i.e. 12 weeks before breaking the news to our family and friends. Usually, when you are 12 weeks pregnant you have your first baby scan at the hospital, where you get the first glimpse of your little one and you know that everything is going well or not.

I had my first baby scan in June 2012. I clearly remember, I was very excited that morning. I took a day off from work. We went to the hospital for the appointment, when my turn came, we both went in to the scan room very excited, I remember we also paid for baby pictures and videos in advance, we did not want to miss out on any little memory of our baby. The scan started and the lady who was doing my baby scan was not satisfied and she took longer than usual to finish my scan whilst also asking me to move, walk, take a break and come back etc. Eventually, the scan ended after three hours, which normally takes thirty minutes. The long process made us suspicious that something was definitely not right. We were asked to wait in the patients waiting area as the senior doctor wanted to come and talk to us. At this point, I started to get worried.

Finally, after an anxious wait the doctor arrived and she took us in a private room. She started the conversation with comforting me first before saying anything related to my scan, by this time I could sense that something dreadful is going to happen. Then she started talking and we got to know that my scan results were indicating towards the likelihood of a high risk of Down Syndrome in the baby, i.e. our baby has a high chance of having Down Syndrome, as high as 1 in 25.

To give a bit of a background about Down Syndrome; In medical science Down syndrome is regarded as a chromosomal disorder where one of the chromosomes have three copies instead of two. The likelihood of an unborn child having Down Syndrome is calculated based on the women's age, first baby scan results and blood tests results. Down Syndrome when serious could mean severe complications with the unborn baby; such as - short life span of the child, physically and mentally impaired, no brain development whatsoever in their lifetime etc. I was low risk as per my age, but my scan results were showing high risk in fact a very high risk, a case of 1 in 25, which was too high. The final test which were left to be done were blood tests, for which the reports would come in after three days which will give a consolidated test result.

Ironically, the doctor who broke the news to us, was also very insensitive towards patients. In 30 minutes of a conservation she told us a number of terrible things that could happen with my baby, such as - baby will die in few years, baby's mental growth will not happen, baby's heart may not work etc. For a first-time 'mother to be', who was carrying a little life inside her hearing such dreadful things regarding her unborn child was a blood-curdling experience. I broke into tears, it felt like my world has shattered, someone just pulled the earth beneath my feet and I was falling into a dark abyss. I didn't have a clue in those moments what we could do to change this, where to go, everything seemed bleak. It all felt unconquerable at the time. Those moments are still so fresh in my mind, while I write this experience it all flashes up again. The doctor also mentioned that expecting parents have a choice to continue or abort the pregnancy.

As I mentioned earlier Down Syndrome if its serious it can mean that there is something horribly wrong with the foetus, which essentially means the child can be mentally and physically impaired, they might not have a heart, will have a short span of life may be about 5-10 years, in short, they obviously cannot live normal lives. Generally, as per the medical science specifications maternal ages of thirty-five and above have a higher chance of having a baby with Down Syndrome, but below that age one is generally safe. As I was only thirty years old at the time, I was put in the safe bucket by doctors. However, as my results were defying all logic, our minds were clouded with negative emotions. We could only think of the worst possibilities that could happen in those moments, despair just overpowered us.

As a result, we started thinking that we should have had the baby earlier. Why did we even wait for so many years! I even lost interest and confidence in having a child anymore. Aimlessly I let them take my blood sample and we left the hospital with a heavy heart for the day. I was completely lost and unclear on what to do next, my tears wouldn't stop even for a minute, my voice just went sore, it was so hard to accept the harsh reality. It was so bizarre that few hours before we were so happy and excited. And now, our lives had gone topsy-turvy and our world literally had gone upside down. The blood results were to arrive after two days. I had a very tough night which seemed like forever. Each moment felt like a huge rock which was unmovable. The next day, I called in to work and took few days off.

The following day I went to a tozo (i.e. chanting with other members) which was held at a member's house in the district, I chanted for the first time after all that has happened with a very heavy mind and heart and with tears all the while. I am short of words to describe how difficult it was. I would not want any mother in this entire world to go through this. I had got to a point where my mind was blank looking straight at the Gohonzon, I never felt that way in my whole life. That day I chanted with no goals, no strategy. After I finished chanting and left that member's place, I had a little light of hope in my heart. I discerned that suddenly something has changed inside me, some of my life force returned and I was able to think logically again. I felt so much better.

I heard the following Gosho lines—

"Each one of you should summon up the courage of a lion king and never succumb to threats from anyone. The lion king fears no other beast, nor do its cubs. Slanders are like barking foxes, but Nichiren's followers are like roaring lions" [WND-1,997].

Practising Nichiren Buddhism empowers us without end. The "courage of a lion king" resides within our own lives. Anyone who chants Nam-myoho-renge-kyo can summon forth that courage without fail. When we brim with the "courage of a lion king" the howling clamour of slander and abuse will not intimidate us. Let's live out our lives with confidence and pride, unbeaten by any trails [Living the Gosho-pg-31].

This guidance stayed with me and in that moment, I decided I was going to chant, chant and chant and I was determined to win, no matter what happens, against all the odds. Some fierce determination came into my life to transform this through chanting. I had no strategy in my mind, I just chanted & chanted. I chanted for the absolute protection of me, my baby and my husband. I chanted for wisdom, life force and courage and the strength to be able to face this difficult circumstance of my life. I chanted to become capable to think and make the right decisions and choose the right path. As I chanted more with this conviction, my faith became even stronger. I started to feel better with each passing hour. I became fearless and deep down I developed unshakeable faith. I started to have faith that whatever happens it's going to be alright, I will be able to take care of it. Whatever happens I surmounted the courage to take responsibility of it. It would be for our good. I developed a life state which was unthinkable for me. I never felt this strong ever before in my life.

Five days later my blood results arrived, it was clear with no issues, my probability of having Downs in my baby went down to 1 in 1000 from 1 in 25. This was my 1st victory. However, these results overcomplicated the situation and made it worse. I had bigger challenges to face because now we had no clarity of why the first scan results showed such a high risk of Down Syndrome. The doctor suggested to do invasive tests to have a 100% confirmation and clarity. Going through the invasive test was the only way to get a 100% clarity. Getting an invasive test meant getting a needle injected in my stomach through which the doctor will take out some fluid and examine it. This would provide 100% accurate results. However, it also meant that there was a 1 % chance of losing your child, because invasive tests can sometimes lead to a miscarriage. Though the chances are rare but because these invasive tests disturbs the equilibrium of the body and the unborn foetus inside, a miscarriage might happen.

At this instant, I had hit another wall. I now had to make this extremely difficult decision. Multiple questions occurred in my mind. On one hand if I make a decision to do the tests and everything goes well, we at least have clarity whether my baby had Downs or not. On the other hand, that what if the baby doesn't have Downs and we go through these tests and while doing it a miscarriage happens? It felt like an impossible decision to make. However, the supreme power of the Mystic Law helped me again. Because I was chanting for wisdom, I decided I will get it done as I need to know. My life was seeking absolute clarity for my unborn child whilst at the same time I was chanting for absolute protection for my baby, myself and my husband. I was literally in a position where no strategy could work, no strategy one could create. This was not about losing a job, or career or money or home. I consider myself to be a reasonably headstrong person and have a fighting spirit when it comes to worldly things such as work, job, money etc. I don't give up easily. I like to try and keep working on it till I achieve what I am aiming for. However, in this situation, I felt completely powerless.

As this was something beyond my control, I could not think of a solution or rather say could not think on what to do. I decided it was important to be patient and trust the power of my faith and my Buddhist practice and the power of the Mystic Law. So instead of trusting my negative thinking mind, I decided to trust and follow the daimoku of faith. When I determined in my heart, my world just opened up to countless possibilities, I received tremendous support from all corners, support just poured in for me. I cannot explain in words, the 'Shoten Zenzins' or protective functions that appeared in my life for my rescue, it was unbelievable. They were all there in every little form, it was miraculous, it felt like the entire universe was supporting me.

I had the good fortune to be with the best consultant, a very experienced and able doctor who did my invasive test at the hospital. His ability was so great that I did not even feel the needle when it went in. He was so accurate, sharp and quick. I have heard horrendous stories about the NHS in the UK, however it all transformed for me. I feel it all happened because of chanting, because daimoku was there in my life. I had managed to change my environment to come for my protection and support. Few days later the results of my invasive tests came in and they turned out to be negative and my baby was declared absolutely 100% safe by the doctors. This was my 2nd victory.

Then there was a third stage to my story, where the doctors still needed to further check that why the first set of results indicated such a high risk of Down Syndrome. They needed to make sure that everything is fine. The last possibility was that there might be a problem with the baby's heart, so my unborn child's heart needed to be checked. Foetus heart check-ups are only done at Great Ormond's street hospital in London, they are an extremely busy hospital and it is near to impossible to get an appointment there at short notice. To my good fortune we got an appointment really quickly, my baby's heart was checked, and it was all fine. The doctors there said that, they were very happy with my baby's heart. They also said that the baby is very active, which when I think about him today is actually true. My son is really active, keeps me on my toes. This was my 3rd victory. I was rest assured and all my fears were put to rest.

I decided to be a votary of the Lotus Sutra for life, to embrace the Lotus Sutra for life. Daimoku can do wonders for one's life. I received my Gohonzon in August 2012 after all my tests were completed. My son was born absolutely healthy and happy in December 2012. I received tremendous support from all members of my district and leaders at the time in all my struggles. It was such a healing experience. I was truly grateful to the universe for bringing me closer to the Gohonzon, the Mystic Law and for my new loving and caring family of SGI.

I had a tremendously challenging journey raising my son with all kinds of obstacles coming my way. All along the journey this amazing practice became my anchor and a source of fostering unending wisdom and enormous capability in me. I also did a dedicated Lilac activity which is a volunteering activity for two years at Taplow-Court, which is our Buddhist Centre in Maidenhead. In hindsight I believe that activity helped me to develop an immensely capable life state which was just what I needed to handle the trials and tribulations of life, back then and now.

I would briefly like to talk about my most mighty victory throughout this whole journey. After I had my first child and I emerged out victorious from that situation, I was immensely grateful to the universe and the practice. However, I also thought I would never put myself through this ever again. The fear and the repercussions of that whole situation never left my heart. I always thought it was our good fortune and the protection of my chanting that it all had gone well. But it could also have been a coincidence. I always wanted to have a second child but could never gather the courage to imagine even thinking about it. As a result of my first experience, it's only natural to think in that manner. However, as I was chanting and reading the Gosho all this while wisdom prevailed.

I read the following Gosho lines-

"So long as one maintains firm faith, one is certain to receive the great protection of the gods. I say this for your sake. I know your faith has always been admirable, but now you must strengthen it more than ever" [WND-1,614].

The human heart is a wondrous thing. We can strengthen and deepen our heart without limit. And faith is its strongest and deepest expression. No matter what our circumstances may be, when we have firm faith in the Mystic Law, we will definitely be protected by the positive functions of the universe. In Nichiren Buddhism faith means always looking to the future and making a fresh start from this moment on. Let's being each day anew with the resolve to strengthen our faith more than ever. This is the essence of the proud ever-victorious spirit of the SGI [Living the Gosho-pg-57].

I determined to make a fresh start and I gradually summoned up the courage to come out of this fear, think fearlessly indistinct of the past and take responsibility of my life. I took the plunge of going for a second child. It was a very liberating and empowering experience to make that decision, to be fearless. The second time my journey was uniquely incredibly challenging in its own way. My personal health suffered massively. I went through phases of depressive moods pre and post pregnancy. I experienced life's realities in earnestness, had deep insights about all my relationships like a clear mirror, harsh but true realities and I must say all for a good reason. At many levels, I experienced the meaning of the Gosho line 'casting off the transient and revealing the true'. I learnt a great deal about the profoundness of life during this whole journey and it was all because of chanting, studying about Nichiren Buddhism and doing activities within SGI.

As I was following all the three pillars of this profound practice i.e. faith, practice and study. I had the good fortune of becoming a mother again for a second time to another beautiful baby boy. He is like the gift of heaven filled with preciousness and purity. I am a very proud mother of my two boys and an immensely proud practitioner of Nichiren Buddhism.

The enormous thing which happens when one's going through stressful times is that one cannot think clearly. Panic takes over and negative thoughts overpowers our minds, hence thinking rationally about a conclusion seems impossible. The virtue of wisdom vanishes away, leaving human beings submerged with evil thoughts. No responsible actions can be taken in such a life state. It is the life state which gets consumed by the situation.

However, when we chant daimoku, wisdom, clarity and courage prevail. It is wonderous and mystic. Chanting Nam-myoho-renge-kyo helped me determine, decide and think correctly. It instilled a profound wisdom in me to think clearly for a solution and also take actions to achieve it. It also enabled me to maintain peace within my body, mind and soul. It is indeed an incredibly precious state of life when you have unshakeable faith in yourself. Such a life state comes alive through having unwavering faith in the practice that one can overcome anything. We can absolutely transform any situation to our benefit and turn any poison into medicine. When we chant with this conviction, Buddhahood emerges from within and flows like a gentle stream guiding and supporting us along the way. We align ourselves with the rhythm of our inherent nature and the universe. The forces in the universe aligns too and everything's starts to work in accordance.

I have immense gratitude for this practice and I am a votary of the Lotus Sutra for life. With this vow in my heart I determine to become absolutely happy and support others do the same. This is the year 2019 when I write this experience and I have two beautiful boys aged six and nearly three. I will truly be grateful to the universe if my story gives you hope in your struggles.

I would like to end with the following–

The Daishonin writes: 'The greater the hardships befalling [the votary of the Lotus Sutra], the greater the delight he feels, because of his strong faith' (WND-1, 33).

When we have strong faith, encountering obstacles can serve to strengthen our conviction in the validity of Nichiren Buddhism and bring us joy. The phrase in the Lotus Sutra 'living beings enjoy themselves at ease' (LSOC16, 272) doesn't mean not having any difficulties. It means establishing a state of life in which we are fearless, no matter what happens, and are able to overcome every obstacle with confidence and composure, savouring the joy of faith in our hearts each day. "With ever stronger faith, let's enjoy life, free of fear, while receiving boundless benefits!" [NHR, Vol-27, Chapter-3, Fierce Struggle-1].

Seiko's Experience

I moved to UK from Japan in 2008 to live with my British husband, whom I met while he was working in a town in Osaka where I lived. Six months later, we married at Taplow Court. I was the happiest woman in the world.

I immediately wanted to have a baby. My husband didn't. He wanted me to settle in UK first, which meant I needed to improve my English and get a job. When I look back at the time, I think I was seeking my role here in UK, but I was not confident about getting a job or making friends whom I could speak to in English. I thought the easiest option to fill up my lack of confidence, was to become a mother. My husband wanted me to become an independent, strong woman. And I suffered pressure from his image of an ideal woman. For me, the strong female figure was far from myself at that time. I chanted every day for almost 3 hours to find a job as I didn't have anything to do but chanting. And eventually I found the job I chanted for. Gradually my English improved and I became more confident and felt secure living in UK, forgetting about having a family. I enjoyed myself here.

After a couple of years since we married, friends around us started having babies and we were so happy to meet their little ones. Gradually, we wanted to have our own. We finally felt we were ready for a family! We both thought as soon as we try, I would get pregnant. But the reality was I didn't. I started feeling jealous when I heard the news that somebody we knew had gotten pregnant.

2 years later, we started seeking medical advice. The GP referred us to the hospital, but we didn't hear anything for 3 months. I called up the hospital and they said our names were not on the list. It turned out that the GP had got a wrong fax number for the referral! We had to wait for another 3 months. In 2013 we finally got a hospital appointment. From the examination, we found out that my left fallopian tube was blocked, so my chance of getting pregnant was lower than those women who haves both tubes unblocked. Plus, I had low egg counts.

My husband immediately looked into IVF. I wasn't sure what to do. We visited a couple of private clinics and attended introductory sessions for IVF. I was not sure whether what we were trying to do was right for me. Wasn't it my ego that I wanted to have a child? I thought a lot about life itself.

Don't get me wrong. I don't have any objection with anyone who goes in for IVF and I would recommend IVF or other medical treatments available if anyone suffers from infertility. However, I could not settle my feelings towards IVF. But my husband was really keen to try it. My husband asked the doctor for the earliest possible IVF treatment date. The doctor said it was in the middle of November 2015. This meant that the result would come before Christmas, which was a few weeks later. I wasn't ready at all. But my husband wanted to try as soon as possible. I could not say anything but yes. I felt guilty of not having a child, because of my infertility.

So, the first cycle of IVF treatment started immediately. At the beginning of December, the festive season started, every weekend, there was a party. We were invited to a Christmas party at our friends' who had a one-year old baby and all the guests were happy talking about their kids and babies.

During that party, I found out that the IVF treatment didn't work. It was very hard to pretend that I was having a good time at the party.

When we got home, I told my husband that IVF failed. I expected that he would sympathise with me and comfort me with compassionate words. Instead, what he said to me was something like "we knew that this result might happen so we can't be disappointed too much." It was hard that I could not share my feelings and talk about it fully with the one person whom I most wanted to share with. (Recently I found out that he also was very disappointed but didn't want to show that to me.)

The next day, there was a family dinner to celebrate my mother in law's birthday. There was my husband's sister who was pregnant with their first baby, and her partner, and my husband's brother and his partner, who were recently engaged, and my parents in law. Just before dinner, my husband's brother announced that they were expecting their baby. The whole family cheered and celebrated the happy news, except me. My heart sunk. I held onto my tears so hard, trying not to cry. I made utmost effort to smile and congratulate them.

The topic at dinner, as I remember, was all about their pregnancy and about how she was coping with her pregnancy. I envied them. I didn't want to go to any other Christmas party at all, after finding out my IVF had failed. But I couldn't say that because failure of IVF is not a miscarriage or anything. I wasn't even pregnant. I can't remember what I said, or who I spoke to at the dinner. All I remember is that I felt so isolated and lonely; nobody knew how broken I was.

When we got home, I didn't know how to deal with the situation I was in. I was devastated. I sat in front of Gohonzon and started to chant. This was the only thing I could do. As soon as I started chanting, all the emotions came out – disappointment, anger, envy and jealousy - towards my husband, my friends, my family, my in-laws, sisters' in law... all the emotions that I tried to hide and didn't want to admit that I carried around appeared. I don't think I've ever been so honest about my feelings to the Gohonzon. I had been chanting for my kosen-rufu baby, but I wasn't sure how earnest the prayer had been. I chanted for it because I thought my prayer should have been linked to kosen-rufu, but my heart was not actually in the prayer.

This time, I chanted and chanted just for my happiness - I didn't want to feel miserable. I wanted to become happy. I wanted to celebrate my sisters in law's pregnancy. I want to feel genuinely happy for them. I didn't want to feel jealous. All I wanted was happiness. That was what I chanted for. But I chanted wholeheartedly.

I don't know how long I chanted but I don't think I chanted long. Suddenly, I felt how fortunate I was to go through this journey. How grateful I was, to encounter this opportunity which would enable me to understand others who were going through the same struggle.

I cried with tears of gratitude for the Gohonzon. Then my prayer shifted. My prayer became a determination that no matter what happens, I will become happy in the end. I may not be able to have a child and would feel miserable or heartbroken for a while, but I decided that I would definitely become happy in the end. Absolute happiness is what Toda Sensei and Ikeda Sensei promised. So why don't I achieve that. It was like the blue sky started spreading in my heart. All the dark clouds of disappointment, anger, jealous and envy were gone.

My husband wanted to try the second cycle of IVF. I didn't feel up to it. I said no to that. I didn't feel guilty about my decision. And he respected my decision. In late February, my husband's sister held her baby shower. I was so happy for her, from the bottom of my heart. So happy to be able to share the moment with her, her friends, my other pregnant sister in law and my mother in law. A week later from then, I found out that I was pregnant.

When we told my mother in law, she said "No wonder you were so merry at the baby shower, because you knew you were pregnant then!" She was surprised when I said that I didn't know that then.

My due date was 6th November 2016. My water broke in early morning on 15th Sep, I was not even on maternity leave. I was admitted to the hospital and there was a concern that my baby's lung was not fully developed yet to be able to breath by herself, if she was born.

Luckily the North London young women's summer course was on that weekend and many members in young women's division chanted for me.

I chanted in the hospital room and talked to my daughter in my heart "do not worry, Mum can protect you." I had no fear.

My daughter was born in the morning of 18th September. She was very tiny but breathing soundly. She had amazing care at NICU and SCBU (special care baby unit) at Whittington hospital. The doctors initially said she might need to stay in the hospital for a month, but she was discharged in 2 weeks. She is now a very healthy 2 year old. And she is to become a big sister in May, this year, which was a total surprise for us.

Having my daughter is amazing. No doubt about that. But what I am most grateful for, is that I could have this experience to deepen my life, so that I can now understand other's suffering what I went through. I now know that I have the power to create happiness by myself no matter what.

To end my experience, I would like to share a Gosho with you;

"Suffer what there is to suffer, enjoy what there is to enjoy. Regard both suffering and joy as facts of life and continue chanting Nam-myoho-renge-kyo, no matter what happens. How could this be anything other than the boundless joy of the Law? Strengthen your power of faith more than ever." (WND I: 86 Happiness in This World, pp.681 - 682).

Thank you very much.

Vidhi's Experience

My name is Vidhi Gupta and I have been practicing for 10 years now. My husband, Siddharth (Sid) and I were married in 2012 and have been very fortunate to both have good careers and a beautiful home in London. We travelled a great deal in the first few years of our marriage and really enjoyed building our relationship, knowing that children were on the horizon, but not immediately.

In 2015, I began to start the conversation with Sid about kids. I faced his reluctance and push back. I felt a bit hurt that he didn't get how my body clock and maternal instincts were kicking in and how I did feel the need to have a child. It led to some discord between us. I chanted for us to be in alignment and eventually in 2016, he reluctantly gave in and we began trying for a baby. It took us a long time to become pregnant and in January 2017 I did test positive. Sid and I were delighted. I felt like the chanting had borne fruit because the Gohonzon had given me what I needed when we were both ready for this baby. Any sooner could have meant Sid wouldn't have been that enthused and that would have been very difficult for us.

The pregnancy progressed with its own challenges. In my very first trimester, I was diagnosed with gestational diabetes and was put on both oral medication and insulin immediately. I really struggled to manage my food, exercise and stress levels to maintain my sugar levels. My work was also stressful and gave me little joy.

My 12-week scan was scheduled on a Saturday afternoon. I woke up that morning knowing that something was not right. I chanted for strength to face the day. Sid and I went into the scan room. The sonographer started the scan and after a few measurements told us that the baby had a thick NT fluid (the fluid that sits behind the baby's neck and a thicker amount is an indication of chromosomal abnormalities). I was instantly in tears and wept as the sonographer finished the scan and sent us for blood works.

The following week was a blur. Further testing confirmed the baby had Down's Syndrome and I wept in-front of the Gohonzon asking for strength, courage and wisdom to make the decisions that were right for my family. Sid was my absolute rock, but I knew he was broken inside.

We made the difficult decision to terminate the pregnancy. Our family in India urged us to come home to Delhi to support us through the ordeal that was to follow. We flew to Delhi in the next few days. I continued to struggle with my grief and with guilt - guilt of being the mother who could not make space in her life to accommodate a child with special needs.

I sought guidance from a senior leader in Delhi and he advised me to chant to the Gohonzon and be grateful for having this child and chant that her short mission may be achieved. In addition to the guidance I received, I also gained a lot of strength from reading a similar experience shared by a fellow member over and over again (https://chantforabetterlife.wordpress.com/2011/05/21/no-prayer-of-the-votary-of-the-lotus-sutra-goes-unanswered/). This gave me strength to know why this baby had come to me and that with the power and protection of the practice, I would be able to heal and move on. I chanted with all my heart and the day I went for my procedure, I was calm knowing that her mission was complete. The procedure was very difficult for me - physically and emotionally. I wept when I saw her tiny little body and am so grateful for the support of family and friends that held us through that time.

I returned to London in May 2017 and threw myself into every distraction I could find - work, learning how to drive, tennis lessons - anything that would help me cope with my grief and guilt. I chanted and got guidance, which helped me to start coming to terms with my loss. I started to accept that I had made the decision which was best for my family and that it came from a place of love for the baby and not wanting her to have a difficult life full of potential surgeries and medication. I began to forgive myself and heal. Sid and I started to try for another baby soon after.

By March 2018, we had not become pregnant and were visiting Delhi again to celebrate my mother-in-law's 60th birthday. At the end of our trip, I visited a doctor for a check-up. The very commercial doctor we met tried very hard to sell us all sorts of treatments, all of which we resisted. At the end she offered a small investigative procedure, one we mystically decided to go for, despite no rationale for doing so. The test revealed that my previous termination had left both my fallopian tubes blocked and I was not going to able to conceive without intervention.

Despite being extremely disappointed with that diagnosis, I was grateful to the Gohonzon that the doctor pushed that procedure and we agreed and were able to find out about my condition, rather than continue to try to get pregnant naturally and fail...only to get frustrated.

I came back to London. Sid and I were dejected. We questioned why we were having to struggle so much to have a baby. I realised the cause of this unhappiness - for the last few years I was tying my happiness to the thought of this baby arriving, rather than enjoying and being grateful for what I had. I chanted to be happy where I was and how I was. And once I began to look at my environment, I had so much to be grateful for and was filled with joy. With this heartfelt gratitude and joy, I chanted. And in a few weeks, I was able to really channel that joy into my daily life and take on the next phase of challenge with determination.

We decided to go through the route of IVF, and opted to have it done in Delhi, to get the support of my parents. I chanted to find the right doctor and clinic. The clinics that were well-recommended and well-known, were very far from where I lived. I needed to be in a clinic close to where I lived, as IVF requires a daily trip. In Delhi, my father took it upon himself to find a clinic. Mystically, he was able to identify flaws/lack of hygiene/too much of a commercial mind-set in several clinics, which he rejected. He finally found a clinic that he was satisfied with, and in June 2018 I flew to Delhi to start my treatment.

My treatment started on the 28th of June. It was my 6th anniversary, and again the practice had taught me to be grateful for all the good fortune I enjoyed. Even though the path was difficult, I had my entire family around me. Even though the treatment was expensive, I had more than adequate means to support it. And even though I felt like my job had not allowed me to progress, I was grateful it was a job that allowed me the space and time to go for this long and difficult treatment.

The initial blood tests from the treatment indicated I had a very low level of a certain hormone (AMH), which meant that I had a low count of ovarian reserve (eggs). The level was shockingly low, almost similar to levels found in post-menopausal women! The doctor did warn that this would mean an even more intensive round of medication and even then, success rates would be low.

I chanted for the right outcome, reminding myself that I was determined to succeed, and that success did not only mean that I would have a baby, but that whatever the outcome, I would thrive and enjoy my life.

The treatment progressed. I was being given 4-5 injections a day. I was fortunate that I had few side effects of such heavy levels of drugs and I was determined to make the most of my time in Delhi by helping my mother de-clutter her house and organise some long overdue renovations in the house, something she felt overwhelmed to do by herself. After three weeks of injections I underwent a small procedure where the doctors extracted eggs from my body, to fertilise outside the body. On average, the doctors expect to extract anywhere between 20-30 eggs and the conversion to embryos is only about 40%. But because of my low AMH levels, the doctors were only able to extract 6 eggs and prepared me to accept that I may get only 1-2 viable embryos.

I came home after my procedure and chanted for those tiny eggs to survive and thrive through the night and convert into healthy embryos. The next day, I rang the hospital and even to their amazement my 6 eggs had converted to 5 healthy (grade 1) embryos! I was delighted and knew that a determined heart could win over anything, however adverse the odds may be.

A few days later the doctor and I decided to implant 2 embryos and freeze the remaining 3. We would know the results after 2 weeks. I continued, in the following weeks, to support my mother and help her pack up the house to prepare for renovation, always believing that my choice to do the treatment in Delhi had a deeper purpose and that supporting my parents was part of my mission. Sensei says, "to feel gratitude towards one's parents may seem like a trivial thing, but this is a mark of true maturity and growth as a human being".

Post the implantation of eggs, the rate of success is not very high, primarily because the doctors can no longer intervene, and it is up to nature to work. I had always begrudged my body and my weight and the complications I had in conceiving. But over the last few weeks, my chanting had made me have gratitude for my own self and recognise how much I was able to do with this body and how much my body had endured during all those treatments, without buckling over. Having this attitude made me kinder to myself, and more relaxed. Two weeks after implantation I took a pregnancy test and was elated to see it was positive!!

My pregnancy progressed well and by the end of August, I came back to London and back to my husband. It had been a long and difficult journey for us both, but we were so grateful to have reached that far. I was able to reach out to the hospital's high-risk pregnancy clinic and had myself enrolled into NHS care. The gestational diabetes came back soon, but I was better prepared for it and took it in my stride.

People often complain about the NHS service during pregnancy, but I have had the most remarkable and attentive care I could possibly have asked for. As I write this, I am now in my third trimester of pregnancy and am looking forward to welcoming our baby in March 2019. The thing I have realised over and over again in the last few years of these trying times has been that having gratitude for what you have, gives you the courage to carry on and win. Happiness cannot be tied to your future. It is today. Having gratitude and lion-hearted determination always enables us to overcome challenges. Sensei puts it simply and says, "those who always have a sense of appreciation and gratitude never reach an impasse in life!"

(Vidhi successfully delivered her beautiful, bonny baby boy in March 2019. Both mother and son are doing very well.)

Yumiko's Experience

I was born in Japan and met Nichiren Buddhism through my mother and grandmother who were already practicing strongly.

I came to London in 2003 to finalize my education to become a professional ballet dancer. After completing my education, I started to look for a job. That time, I was chanting strongly to find a job where I could do my kosen-rufu (which is to create value in society through encouraging oneself and others to become absolutely happy) and that would give me a visa to stay in the UK. As a result, I met my husband. Our relationship went well from the very beginning and we got married 5 months later - this was in 2005. Although he was not interested in practicing Buddhism himself, he understood how important the practice was for me and respected the way SGI President Daisaku Ikeda Sensei lives his life, as well as the SGI members shared goal of kosen-rufu.

My husband and I started to consider creating our family in 2010. A year later, nothing had happened, so we decided to receive basic fertility support. Luckily, the doctor's comments were quite positive, so we both thought that it will happen very soon. However, I was still not pregnant even a year and half after we started receiving the treatment. So, we decided to take the big step to receive an advanced fertility treatment known as IVF - again we both were hopeful. However, a year later, we still didn't get the result we wanted - and during that time, I experienced a physical over-reaction from the treatment (known as OHSS) which required a week-long hospitalisation, and also a miscarriage. Failing to see the result was heart-breaking and I felt a massive frustration each time. However, every time I failed, I received warm and powerful support from many SGI members which enabled me to keep having my faith in the Gohonzon (the scroll we chant to, which acts as a mirror reflection of our full potential) and to trust that my pregnancy would happen soon.

The journey was tough, but the power of daimoku (chanting Nam-myoho-renge-kyo) and the support from others always enabled me to get my hopes back. In fact, every time I failed, my faith became deeper and therefore my hope became bigger. Through these experiences, I realized that Nichiren Buddhism has an incredible power to give us a great strength to immediately get up again and to move forward with hope, however hard the circumstance may be.

In September 2013, I had an opportunity to talk to one of the SGI women's division leaders - she really moved my heart because I felt that she was talking to me from her heart. She told me to chant 'I am the Bodhisattva of the earth, I need this baby to do my kosen-rufu!' She also told me that I MUST have absolute conviction in my prayer, and when I am able to do so, my prayer will definitely be answered. It was on that day that I realised that I had probably never chanted with 100% conviction before and that perhaps there was always a little doubt in my prayer. So, I re-determined that I will have my own child who has a great mission to do kosen-rufu with me, I will trust the Gohonzon 100% and chant without any single doubt!

February 2014, we tried another cycle of treatment - this time at a different clinic. The result was successful. The beginning of my pregnancy went well and during our first scan, we saw our baby's tiny heartbeat and found out that we are having two babies. As soon as the way I chanted changed, my prayer was answered - I felt deep gratitude towards the Gohonzon and everyone who kept supporting me through my journey.

Daimoku is indeed a crucial part of our Buddhist practice. However, if my practice was based on only chanting, I wouldn't have been able to get this far. During my journey, I also realised that how important it was to continue doing activities for kosen-rufu and supporting others. Nichiren Daishonin and our three SGI presidents have never stopped making efforts for kosen-rufu, when they were in the midst of challenges. This has been a source of true inspiration in my life. So, I continued supporting my district, and many other SGI activities. I also graduated after a 2-year commitment to the dedicated lilac group in June. I found great pleasure in doing every kosen-rufu activity and in fact, supporting others always in turn supported me a lot too.

Now back to my pregnancy. After finding out that we are having two babies, my pregnancy seemed to be going well. Then at the 20 weeks scan, the babies' anatomical structures were examined - the result showed normal structures in both babies and we found out that we were having a boy and a girl. We were over the moon. However, at the very end of the appointment, we were told that our daughter was significantly smaller than what she should be. At first, we didn't think that it was serious. However, once we were sent to a specialist, we realised that the situation was much more serious than we initially thought. After a few minutes of examination, we were informed that our daughter's placenta was not functioning properly. Therefore, the blood flow to her was quite poor. Everything the doctor explained was what we didn't want to hear, and she told us that our daughter's heart would probably stop very soon, which made both of us cry. However, as I had constructed such a deep faith through the past four and half years of my journey, I could get up with hope again, immediately, ready to fight this new and, by far, the biggest challenge of my life. My daughter was very small, and I was told that because she was trying so hard her heart was enlarged; but the most important thing for me that time was that she was alive, and that her heart was beating. Whatever the doctor said, there was no way I would give up on her life. I was waiting for her to come for a long time. And she chose me as her mother. I was determined that I would save her life.

That time, I had scans every 2 weeks. Although my daughter was gaining her weight little by little, the situation was not looking good. However, I never gave up hope and continued chanting no matter what. My mother, grandmother, and many members from Japan and in the UK were also sending lots of daimoku for our babies. I would never forget all the warm, powerful support and love that we received.

That time, I thoroughly realised that my mother's side of the family seemed to have a heavy karmic pattern of losing a child. My great-grandmother had lost two of her newborn babies, my grandmother had lost her 26 year old son, and my mother had lost her daughter (my older sister) when she was 36 weeks pregnant and now me. To transform this karma, my mother and grandmother have been chanting so much for last 30 years. What was different in my case, was that all previous deaths were sudden, but my daughter gave me a chance to really challenge the situation, and she chose the time when her mother's faith was strong enough to accept and fight. The experience with my daughter made me deeply realize one of my huge missions - to change this family karma right now, for my daughter and for the future generations of our entire family. Obviously, my son's existence was very big for me - every time I felt his strong kick, I felt that he was telling me and his twin sister to not give up!

Since my daughter's problem was detected, there was an incredible change in my father. He was a person who hated religion intensely. He even hated seeing the Gohonzon, never used the word ' 'pray', and when my brother and I were little, he often said to us that if we became Gakkai members or did any Gakkai activities, he wouldn't accept us as his children. However, during my massive challenge, he often sent me a message saying, ' Don't worry I am praying for you every day.'

Also, my mother told me that he was sitting and putting his hands together in front of the Gohonzon. And more surprisingly, he attended the 'kosen-rufu Gongyo

Ceremony' which was held in Tokyo. It was 3:30am in the UK, but I also joined in from London. Even though we were physically not in the same place, I felt the great power of our united prayer and that our lives became one with my daughter's life for the first time. By seeing this incredible change in my father, I was absolutely confident that my daughter had a huge mission to fulfil in her life.

Two days later, my daughter's heart stopped.

I was certain that power of all daimoku we chanted and we received from others became my daughter's life force - the proof is that in spite of the doctors keep telling us that we'll probably lose her at 20 weeks of my pregnancy, she fought to live until nearly 30 weeks. I will never forget how devastated I was when I heard the news of her death; however, I had no regret as I never gave up hope for her life and fought together with her and my whole family through faith. I was filled with a deep sense of gratitude for having the most profound and precious experience with her that moved so many people's hearts. My father told me later, "I am truly glad that we could pray all together, before she left".

During this journey, my husband, who wasn't practising, was also chanting daimoku with me almost every day. We started from chanting Nam-myoho-renge-kyo three times and then chanted continuously for 2-3 minutes by the end. We shared struggles, supported and encouraged one another, and found hope together. Even though my daughter didn't make it into this world, I am certain that she fulfilled her mission to unite my family.

November 2014 (2 months after our daughter's death), our beautiful son arrived safely in perfect health. And we had a beautiful little ceremony to scatter our daughter's ashes together with her twin brother at Taplow Court (the SGI UK National Centre), and there we re-determined not to give up our shared dream of having two children. We prayed sincerely to meet our daughter again in this lifetime.

When my son was 10 months old, we went back to the IVF clinic where I had conceived. Again, the process of the treatment meant a huge physical impact on my body which required about 10 days of hospitalization. However, since the first treatment was successful at this clinic, we had high expectations that we would become pregnant quickly.

The first trial was negative. However, with encouragement and sincere support from SGI members I was able to quickly get my hopes back and keep going. One passage from Gosho (letters of support from Nichiren Daishonin to his disciples) states,

"Those who believe in the Lotus Sutra are as if in winter, but winter always turns to spring." This reassured me that there would definitely be enlightenment in the end. The second trial was negative. It was indeed frustrating. At that point, I questioned if I had 100% conviction in my prayers, and if I was making enough efforts to have this dream come true. The answer was 'No'. Ikeda Sensei taught me "...whether or not we can attain Buddhahood hinges on the strength of our faith. No matter what painful trials we encounter, we must not harbour doubts in our hearts". I re-determined that 'I will chant with the conviction that I will meet my daughter again because she has the mission to do kosen-rufu with me!'

Then the third trial - it was negative again. But as I deepened my faith in the practice and gained a strong fighting spirit over the years, I had the courage not to be defeated, to absolutely win over this situation. I decided to just continue chanting and supporting many SGI activities no matter what. In turn I received incredible support from others - I was not alone.

My father kept supporting me during this period too; every time I reported the results to him, he encouraged me with Buddhist-like words such as 'I trust that your daughter will come back when the time is right'. He also attended several events hosted by SGI, which he said were "very impressive and touching." I also saw a big difference in his attitude towards me - now he listens to me with more sincerity and he often tells me how much hope I've brought into the family.

I recently realised that it is not just my father who has changed through this journey. I, too, have changed. My heart has changed through transforming my negative aspects through Buddhist practice and he simply is mirroring this back to me. I also realized that now, I believe in his Buddha nature and can sincerely pray for his happiness.
There were some moments when I thought ' having one healthy child was the happiest result for our family.' At the same time, my honest feeling was I still couldn't give up on my hope to meet my daughter again. So, we determined to try once again. This time we felt our determination was crucial. I increased my daimoku significantly and chanted with even stronger conviction and did literally everything I could think of, to increase the chance of success.

Then the final trial... the result was, successful! On our 12th anniversary! As soon as my attitude towards facing the challenge changed, my dream manifested, and it was a girl.

During the pregnancy, I challenged myself to take the SGI Grade 3 exam which deepened my relationship with my mentor. Also, as a district leader I shared the joy of practising Nichiren Buddhism with my district members, and 2 new young women received Gohonzon.

3 weeks before the due date I felt that my daughter's movements were reduced and therefore I went to hospital to see if my daughter was ok. Then I was told that it is best to deliver her on that same day. It was totally unexpected. We planned for my husband to stay with me during the labour and my mother to fly from Japan to look after our son. I was not ready, and never thought it would be possible to give birth without anyone's help - all my fears came up in that moment. However, I started to chant strongly in my heart, and I could quickly acquire Buddha's three virtues of courage, wisdom and compassion - I saw the proof of my practice once again. I told my husband to contact his sister who lives in Norway immediately. Normally, she would not be available on weekdays. But somehow, she was taking time off from work and was able to fly to England straight away.

Meanwhile, I contacted our beloved women's division leader (the same person who gave me guidance/encouragements just before conceiving my son), who had a great relationship with our son and also deeply connected with our lost daughter's life. This extremely busy woman was also mystically free that day and next few days to help us. I was admitted to hospital immediately in order to start the induction of labour. It had progressed very quickly. The women's division leader did evening gongyo and some daimoku for the safe delivery and I joined in as much as I could.

The hospital was short of professional staff that day and even though the intervals of the strong contractions became very short, midwives still could not come to me. I was almost unconscious by then but felt that my daughter wanted to come out now. I told the women's division leader. She ran to the midwives and finally they came! My daughter arrived 10 minutes later. The whole process took 36 hours when I had my son, but only 7 hours with my daughter. Without her having stayed with me the whole time, I wouldn't have been able to deliver my daughter safely. We can never fully thank all the support we received from family-like SGI friends and the protection we received from the power of Nam-myoho-renge-kyo. In addition, because our daughter arrived nearly 3 weeks early, I could attend the 'Generation Hope' event (the event that the Youth Division of SGI-UK organized to demonstrate the responsibility of youth to transform the world for the better).

My daughter is another healthy baby, who's been bringing immeasurable happiness into our entire family together with her brother. I truly believe that this is the brave girl who I said goodbye to, 4 years ago.

Until 8 years ago, my practice was quite passive compared to now. Perhaps I was dependent on my mother's prayers. However, through facing the big challenge of my life, I stood up on my own and took responsibility for my own life, by taking actions as a Buddhist practitioner. One realisation was my tendency to become dependent on others, or to seek hope externally. However, the environment or situation will never change unless my heart realises that everything begins from my concrete determination and strong prayer. Having two beautiful children now, is of course my conspicuous benefit, but being able to fundamentally change my negativities has been a tremendous inconspicuous benefit.

Through this 8-year journey, I started to see a new path for my future – I began to study a bachelor's degree in biology, with the dream of working in the field where I could somehow help those people struggling to conceive. I have now applied for a master's degree starting this autumn. From a professional dancer to a scientist, the hardships waiting for me might be beyond my imagination. But I am determined!

Even though life became busier after having children, I always create time to join meetings. I feel true joy involving my children in SGI activities. I am determined to become a mother whose way of living can be a good example. I want them to live an absolutely happy life.

I would like to conclude my experience with Ikeda Sensei's words.
'Difficulty makes us stronger. Great hardships strengthen our faith. If we keep challenging obstacles and forging strong, invincible faith, we can bring forth the state of Buddhahood in our lives'.

Detailed Glossary

Below are some words/terms/phrases/names you may have come across while reading the experiences[2].

Buddhahood
Daimoku
Daisaku Ikeda
Gohonzon
Gongyo
Human Revolution
Josei Toda
Karma
Kosen-rufu
Lotus Sutra
Nam-myoho-renge-kyo
Nichiren Daishonin
Shakubuku
Shakyamuni
Soka Gakkai International
Three pillars of "Faith, Practice and Study"
Tozo
Tsunesaburo Makiguchi

Buddhahood[3]: Buddhahood isn't some transcendental state of life that is separate from daily reality. Buddhahood means enlightenment – enlightened to the true nature and potential of life. As such, it is a state of life which each individual inherently possesses. The awakening of this state in our lives brings with it such characteristics as strengthened life-force, courage, determination, compassion and wisdom.

---

2 *Source: https://sgi-uk.org/ and https://www.sgi.org/about-us/buddhist-concepts/*

3 *http://www.sgm.org.my/en/?cur=page/page&id=197&title=What_is_Buddhahood?*

'Step'n Sea'

5 mins walk from St Ives Station
(Leaves from London Paddington)

2 mins to Beaches / Shops

With regret, no Children or Pets.

Please book through our agents: '**Aspects Holidays**'
Click on '**St Ives Town**' Property **Type in STEP**
Then **'Check Availability'**

Michael and Julia (owners) may be able to
offer some reduction in off-peak seasons
Try: simmo.m@blueyonder.co.uk

'Step'n Sea'

A stylish hide-away for 2 (or 1) in Central St Ives.

• **4 Beaches** •

• Breathtaking Walks •

• **Own Private Parking** •

• Barbara Hepworth Garden •

• **Interesting Shops** •

• Art •

• **Great Restaurants** •

• Tate Gallery •

"Best Seaside Town in Britain"

The Guardian 2007

Daimoku: Chanting Nam-myoho-renge-kyo

Daisaku Ikeda: Daisaku Ikeda is a Buddhist philosopher, peacebuilder, educator, author and poet. He is the third president of the Soka Gakkai and the founding president of the Soka Gakkai International (SGI).

Ikeda was born in Tokyo, Japan, on January 2, 1928, the fifth of eight children, to a family of seaweed farmers. The devastation and senseless horror he witnessed as a teenager during World War II gave birth to a lifelong passion to work for peace, rooting out the fundamental causes of human conflict.

In 1947, at the age of 19, he met Josei Toda (1900–58), educator and leader of the Soka Gakkai. Ikeda found in Toda an open and unaffected person, a man of unshakable conviction with a gift for explaining profound Buddhist concepts in logical, accessible terms. He soon found employment at one of Toda's companies and later completed his education under the tutelage of Toda, who became his mentor in life.

In May 1960, two years after Toda's death, Ikeda, then 32, succeeded him as president of the Soka Gakkai. Under his leadership, the movement began an era of innovation and expansion, becoming actively engaged in cultural and educational endeavours worldwide. Ikeda has dedicated himself to fulfilling Toda's dreams by developing initiatives in the areas of peace, culture and education.

The central tenet of Ikeda's thought, and of Buddhism, is the fundamental sanctity of life, a value which Ikeda sees as the key to lasting peace and human happiness. In his view, global peace relies ultimately on a self-directed transformation within the life of the individual, rather than on societal or structural reforms alone. This idea is expressed most succinctly in a passage in his best-known work, The Human Revolution, Ikeda's novelization of the Soka Gakkai's history and ideals: "A great inner revolution in just a single individual will help achieve a change in the destiny of a nation and, further, will enable a change in the destiny of all humankind."

Gohonzon: The literal meaning is the "object of devotion". Nichiren Daishonin himself described the Gohonzon as 'the object of devotion for observing the mind' meaning that with this object we are able to see all of the ten worlds[4] working in our lives, including the enlightened world of Buddhahood.

---

[4] *https://www.sgi.org/about-us/buddhist-concepts/ten-worlds.html*

The scroll is inscribed with Chinese and Sanskrit characters. SGI members enshrine it in their homes and focus on it when chanting.

Second president of the Soka Gakkai, Josei Toda, would sometimes refer to the Gohonzon as a machine for producing happiness. By this he meant that people bring their sufferings, their problems and desires and chant about them in front of the Gohonzon.

Through the process of raising our life-condition and revealing our enlightened life, we are able to see our lives from the Buddha's perspective. This means that we view our desires and problems differently and are able to change from seeking relative happiness to revealing the joy of our absolute happiness from within.

Gongyo: The Japanese word gongyo means "assiduous practice"— gon indicates "exertion," "diligence," "assiduousness"; gyo means "to carry out."[5]

In the SGI, our assiduous practice consists of chanting Nam-myoho-renge-kyo and reciting portions of "Expedient Means" (the 2nd chapter of the Lotus Sutra) and "Life Span of the Thus Come One" (the sutra's 16th chapter) every morning and evening with faith in the Gohonzon. Chanting Nam-myoho-renge-kyo is the "primary practice," while reciting the sutra is called the "supplementary practice."

Gongyo is a short ceremony which enables us to celebrate our inherent Buddhahood and offer prayers of gratitude and determination for whatever is relevant to us at any particular time.

Human Revolution: Human Revolution is the idea that the inner transformation of an individual will cause a positive change in one's circumstances and ultimately in society as a whole.

Human revolution brings into play all the principles and processes that make up the Buddhist teachings of life. Learning to be able to live our lives on the basis of correct teachings is part of our human revolution. The process is a transformation of the heart.
When we commit our lives to chanting, we embark on a journey of self-discovery and challenge. By taking responsibility for our feelings and emotions, especially those we most dislike, we come to realise we have the ability to transform our lives

---

5 https://www.worldtribune.org/2016/10/q-a-on-gongyo/

from within. As we broaden our experiences of chanting daimoku we get experiences of our environment reflecting the transformation of our inner lives. This could be in our family relationships, at work or in other aspects of life.

In his book For the Sake of Peace, Daisaku Ikeda talks about human revolution in terms of self-mastery. Simply put, this means winning control over oneself, overcoming the small self that is dominated by narrow self-interest and awakening to the larger self that works for the good of all humanity. From this standpoint a major obstacle to developing ourselves is to pursue a way of life bound by our small ego or self. Expanding from the lesser self to the greater self is the path of human revolution.

Josei Toda (1900–58): Josei Toda was an educator, publisher and entrepreneur and the served as the second president of the lay Buddhist organisation, the Soka Gakkai.

After his release from prison at the end of World War II, Toda began to reconstruct the collapsed Soka Kyoiku Gakkai, renaming it the Soka Gakkai (Society for the Creation of Value).

Toda taught that through Buddhist practice and inner-motivated change, or "human revolution," all people can change their destiny for the better. This message resonated powerfully among the many people suffering from poverty, illness and other challenges in the chaos of post-war Japan. Moreover, Toda's unshakeable confidence in the power of Nichiren's philosophy and his ability to translate the profound concepts of Buddhism into practical guidance for daily life re-ignited people's hope and courage.

By the time of his death in 1958, Toda had built an organization of nearly one million members and laid the foundation for the dramatic spread of Nichiren Buddhism in Japan and abroad.

Karma: Originally the Sanskrit word 'karma' meant 'action' or 'act'. In time, it came to imply deeds or results.

It is important to recognise that karma can be both positive and negative, and it is certainly good karma to have been born a human being. Most often, however, people are more likely to think about karma in a negative way. When this expression is misused it can take on the appearance of referring to some fixed 'fate' or 'destiny' which is absolutely not what it is about in Nichiren Buddhism. Rather than being the judgement of some external force, Nichiren Buddhism clarifies the importance of an individual's free will.

If we are responsible for creating our personal karma, then we are also able to change it. It is of course important to recognise that everyone's karma is different.

The Buddhist principle of karma can help us understand what we can do to break out of the repetitive patterns that might cause ourselves and others suffering. The power and force of our inherent Buddhahood is greater and stronger than the karma we created in the past. The process of changing our karma is not merely to eradicate the negative from our lives.

Daisaku Ikeda explains:
We don't focus on our karma merely so that we may repay our 'karmic debt' and bring our 'balance' to zero. Rather it is to convert our 'negative balance' into a large 'positive balance'. This is the principle of changing karma in Nichiren Buddhism. And it is the Buddha nature existing in the lives of all people that makes this possible. Our focus on changing karma is backed by our steadfast belief in our own Buddha nature.

Kosen-rufu: The Japanese phrase kosen-rufu expresses a centrally important concept for members of the SGI. It is often used synonymously with world peace and has been informally defined as "world peace through individual happiness." More broadly, it could be understood as a vision of social peace brought about by the widespread acceptance of core values such as unfailing respect for the dignity of human life.

Thus, for the members of the SGI, kosen-rufu means the ceaseless effort to enhance the value of human dignity, to awaken all people to a sense of their limitless worth and potential. It is for this reason that efforts in the fields of peace, humanitarian aid, educational and cultural exchange are all seen as vital aspects of the movement for kosen-rufu. For these promote the values that are integral to human happiness.

Finally, it should be understood that kosen-rufu does not represent a static end point. As SGI President Daisaku Ikeda noted in 1970, "Kosen-rufu does not mean the end point or terminus of a flow, but it is the flow itself, the very pulse of living Buddhism within society."

The stress placed by Nichiren on kosen-rufu typifies his approach to Buddhist practice; that our personal happiness—enlightenment—is inextricably linked with the peace and happiness of our fellow humans and of society as a whole.

In this sense, the "attainment" of kosen-rufu does not suggest the end of history or of the inevitable conflicts and contradictions that drive history. Rather, it could be thought of as building a world in which a deeply and widely held respect for human life would serve as the basis on which these can be worked out in a peaceful, creative manner. This is not something, however, which we must passively wait for.

Buddhism teaches that it is something that we can begin to implement right now, wherever we are.

Lotus Sutra: The Lotus Sutra is widely regarded as one of the most important and influential sutras, or sacred scriptures, of Buddhism. In it, Shakyamuni expounds the ultimate truth of life to which he was enlightened. The sutra's key message is that Buddhahood, the supreme state of life characterized by boundless compassion, wisdom and courage, is inherent within every person without distinction of gender, ethnicity, social standing or intellectual ability.

The Lotus Sutra is a teaching that encourages an active engagement with mundane life and all its challenges. Buddhahood is not an escape from these challenges but an inexhaustible source of positive energy to grapple with and transform the sufferings and contradictions of life and create happiness. As SGI President Daisaku Ikeda has written, the Lotus Sutra is ultimately a teaching of empowerment. It "teaches us that the inner determination of an individual can transform everything; it gives ultimate expression to the infinite potential and dignity inherent in each human life."

Nam-myoho-renge-kyo: Nam-myoho-renge-kyo is the teaching for ordinary people to reveal their greatest potential. The simplest translated meaning is "I devote my life to the Mystic Law of cause and effect."

Nam-myoho-renge-kyo is a vow, an expression of determination, to embrace and manifest our Buddha nature. It is a pledge to oneself to never yield to difficulties and to win over one's suffering. At the same time, it is a vow to help others reveal this law in their own lives and achieve happiness.

The individual characters that make up Myoho-renge-kyo express key characteristics of this law:

Nam comes from the Sanskrit namas, meaning to devote or dedicate oneself.

Myo can be translated as mystic or wonderful, and **ho** means law.

Renge, meaning lotus blossom, is a metaphor that offers further insight into the qualities of this Mystic Law. The lotus is a common symbol in Buddhism because it is a beautiful plant that grows in the muddy swamp. This encourages us to recognise that the real place of Buddhist practice is not secluded away from the realities of life, in a monastery or a convent, or on a mountain top, but is rooted in society, in the real life that we ordinary people experience. The lotus is also one of a small number of plants which produce flowers and fruit at the same time (rather than as more commonly happens, blossom appearing before fruit which contains seeds). This means that the lotus can be used to symbolise the principle of the simultaneity of cause and effect, which is particularly relevant for the idea of revealing Buddhahood in this lifetime. The action which is the cause to reveal our Buddhahood has an instantaneous effect; we don't have to wait to see our Buddhahood emerge.

Kyo literally means 'sutra' or 'teaching'. The character that is used to write this also implies the warp of cloth, and implies that all phenomena are interconnected, not only in the present, but also in the past and future. Because traditionally a teaching was transmitted orally, this character also resonates with the importance of sound and vibration, activity we see throughout the universe. 'Kyo' informs us that all phenomena are manifestations of the Mystic Law.
To chant Nam-myoho-renge-kyo is an act of faith in the Mystic Law and in the magnitude of life's inherent possibilities.

While this phrase explains the workings of life (almost as a scientific formula does), it was Nichiren Daishonin's intention that we should more deeply understand that this phrase is the name of the Buddha potential in our lives. The purpose of Buddhism is to enable us to reveal our greatest potential, and Nichiren Daishonin recognised the power of this phrase to enable us to do that.

The name of the Buddha nature, the ninth consciousness, is Nam-myoho-renge-kyo. If we call its name, we will stimulate and activate the ninth consciousness and it will emerge from within us. Nichiren Daishonin wrote: 'When we revere Myoho-renge-kyo inherent in our own life as the object of devotion, the Buddha nature within us is summoned forth and manifested by our chanting of Nam-myoho-renge-kyo.

Nichiren Daishonin (1222–82): the priest who established the form of Buddhism practiced by the members of the SGI, is a unique figure in Japanese social and religious history. An outspoken critic of the established Buddhist schools and the secular authorities, he was also a person of great warmth and humanity, as is evident in the content of the numerous letters he sent to his followers. It was this deep concern for the welfare of ordinary people that made him such an unrelenting opponent of the often corrupt and oppressive social structures of his time.

Over a thousand years after Shakyamuni, amidst the turbulence of 13th-century Japan, Nichiren similarly began a quest to recover the essence of Buddhism for the sake of the suffering masses. Awakening to the law of life himself, Nichiren was able to discern that this fundamental law is contained within Shakyamuni's Lotus Sutra and that it is encapsulated and concisely expressed in the sutra's title—Myoho-renge-kyo. Nichiren designated the title of the sutra as the name of the law and established the practice of reciting Nam-myoho-renge-kyo as a practical way for all people to focus their hearts and minds upon this law and manifest its transformative power in reality.

Nichiren spread the teaching of Nam-myoho-renge-kyo, providing the means for people to free themselves from suffering at the most fundamental level. It was after this that he began to inscribe the Gohonzon for his followers—a scroll inscribed with Chinese characters that embodies the Mystic Law to which he was enlightened.

Shakubuku: The act of introducing others to Buddhism, which enables us to profoundly benefit both ourselves and others, is the formula of hope for humanity. Through our practice of introducing others to Nichiren Daishonin's Buddhism, and through efforts to share Buddhism with others, we ourselves grow immensely, we can carry out our human revolution, and transform our karma. Therefore, by guiding another individual towards happiness, we also guide ourselves towards happiness.

Shakyamuni: Buddhism originates with Shakyamuni (also known as Gautama or Siddhartha), who was born in what is now Nepal, some 2,500 years ago, into a royal family. Shakyamuni, from a young age, became aware of and was profoundly troubled by the problems of human suffering. Buddhist scriptures describe four encounters which served to awaken in him an awareness of four sufferings common to all people—birth, aging, sickness and death. This pre-occupation with sufferings was the trigger for him to embark on a spiritual quest to become enlightened to the true nature of life.

For several years, he subjected himself to ascetic practices but found these did not offer a way forward. Taking a middle way, he entered a profound meditation. There he attained an awakening, or enlightenment, to the true nature of life and all things, including human suffering. It was because of this enlightenment that he came to be called Buddha, or "Awakened One."

Soka Gakkai International: The Soka Gakkai International (SGI) is a community-based Buddhist organization that promotes peace, culture and education centred on respect for the dignity of life. SGI members uphold the humanistic philosophy of Nichiren Buddhism in 192 countries and territories around the world.

Individual SGI members strive to actualize their inherent potential while contributing as empowered global citizens to their local communities and responding to the shared issues facing humankind. The SGI's efforts to help build a lasting culture of peace are based on a commitment to dialogue and non-violence, and the understanding that individual happiness and the realization of a peaceful world are inextricably linked.

As a nongovernmental organization with formal ties to the United Nations, the SGI also collaborates with other civil society organizations, intergovernmental agencies and faith groups in the fields of nuclear disarmament, human rights education, sustainable development and humanitarian relief.

SGI members integrate Buddhist practice into the daily rhythm of their lives. They aim to develop and strengthen their lives through chanting Nam-myoho-renge-kyo and by studying the teachings of Buddhism.

The basic morning and evening practice, known as gongyo, consists of chanting Nam-myoho-renge-kyo and reciting portions of the Lotus Sutra. This is usually carried out at home but can also be done together with others.

The aim of this practice is to develop one's Buddha nature--the qualities of courage, wisdom and compassion--thereby tapping the energy needed to tackle one's challenges, transform one's life and contribute to the happiness of others. In countries where there is an SGI organization, members and guests meet to share experiences of their practice and study together at regular monthly discussion meetings. Practice naturally leads to a sense of empowerment and responsibility, and SGI members aim to positively impact the communities in which they live.

A scholar recently noted that one reason the SGI has attracted such a diverse group of people over the years is that it emphasizes and encourages people to apply Buddhist practice to winning in their lives. This accords with Nichiren's emphasis on actual results as the most reliable gauge of the validity of a Buddhist teaching. As he says, "Nothing is more certain than actual proof" ("The Teaching, Practice, and Proof," WND-1, 478).[6]

Three pillars of Faith, Practice and Study

> **Faith:** Faith means to have absolute conviction that our prayers to the Gohonzon (object of devotion) and our practice of Nichiren teachings will enable us to achieve a life of great happiness and fulfilment without fail.[7]

> To elaborate, 'faith' in Nichiren Buddhism essentially means firm belief in the Mystic Law of cause and effect that governs all phenomena. Faith could be described as the ongoing effort to orient one's heart toward the ideal of Buddhahood—the continual unfolding of one's inherent potential for good, the ability to transform any negative circumstance into a source of growth and benefit, and a life dedicated toward helping others do the same.

> **Practice:** Practice refers to the actions that express our faith and to further develop it. It comprises practice for oneself and practice for others[8].

> Practice for oneself is the daily practice of offering prayers to the Gohonzon. It involves chanting the phrase "Nam-myoho-renge-kyo" and reciting excerpts from two important chapters of the Lotus Sutra.

> Practice for others refers to the act of introducing others to Nichiren Buddhism based on the Buddhist compassion to enable others to attain happiness. It also encompasses the participation in various activities of faith organized by Soka Gakkai.

---

[6] *https://www.sgi-usa.org/study-resources/core-concepts/faith-equals-daily-life/*

[7] *https://ssabuddhist.org/philosophy-and-practice/faq/#.XMwLgehKhPY*

[8] *https://ssabuddhist.org/philosophy-and-practice/faq/#.XMwLgehKhPY*

Study: Nichiren Daishonin encouraged us to study so that we will understand what is happening to us as we undergo the process of moving our lives in the direction we have chosen.

In the SGI, there are three main sources of study material
1. The Lotus Sutra which forms the basis of Nichiren Buddhism
2. The writings of Nichiren Daishonin as outlined in letters to his disciples in a book called the Gosho
3. The guidance and encouragement from SGI President Daisaku Ikeda

Tozo: A tozo is a meeting where members chant daimoku together.

Tsunesaburo Makiguchi (1871–1944): a reformist educator, author and philosopher who founded the Soka Kyoiku Gakkai (the forerunner of the Soka Gakkai) in 1930. His life was characterized by confrontation with repressive authorities.

As a teacher known for his warmth and consideration, he strove to introduce a more humanistic, student-centred approach to education. He fiercely opposed corrupt educational practices and was forced into early retirement as a result. Later, he was imprisoned for opposing the policies of the Japanese militarist regime. He died in prison from malnutrition at the age of 73. In recent years his humanistic educational theories have been attracting increasing international attention.

Frequently Asked Questions[9]

What Buddhist tradition is SGI part of?

SGI members embrace Nichiren Buddhism, following a Lotus Sutra-based practice formulated by the 13th-century Japanese priest Nichiren. The Lotus Sutra is considered by many in the Mahayana Buddhist tradition to be the fullest expression of the teachings of Shakyamuni, the historical Buddha who was born in present-day Nepal some 2,500 years ago.

The Lotus Sutra is revered for its embracing message that all people possess the Buddha nature, both men and women. The image of the pure lotus flower growing in a muddy pond symbolizes how people can develop this enlightened state of life in the midst of their daily problems and struggles.

Nichiren studied all available Buddhist texts and investigated the many competing schools of Buddhism of his day before concluding that the Lotus Sutra epitomized the true compassionate intent of Shakyamuni. Today, SGI members study the letters and treatises of Nichiren and his analysis of the Lotus Sutra, as well as the Lotus Sutra itself and commentaries by SGI President Daisaku Ikeda.

Do SGI members have to follow rules?

There are no set rules that regulate the lives of SGI members, but they are encouraged to live constructive lives and to respect the laws and norms of the societies and cultures in which they live.

Based on conviction in the dignity and inherent worth of all human beings, as taught in the Lotus Sutra, individuals are trusted to develop the ability to see the true nature of their thoughts, words and actions, and the wisdom to make the right choices for their lives. Practicing Buddhism naturally leads one to refrain from denigrating and destroying life and to wish to support and encourage others.

The SGI Charter lays out the broad goals of the organization and its vision of contributing to a peaceful, just and sustainable world based on the principles of Nichiren Buddhism.

---

[9] *https://www.sgi.org/faq/*

What are the benefits of practicing Buddhism with other people?

The practice of Buddhism focuses not just on benefiting and developing oneself, but on the needs of others as well. Through exchange, dialogue and contact, people at any stage of their practice can learn more than they can by practicing in isolation. Newcomers are always encouraged to raise questions.

Buddhist practice is not easy, requiring self-discipline, and seeing one's own life clearly can be tough--this is why support from others is important as people strive to bring out their highest potential. Through the extensive network of the SGI organization, people can receive encouragement, build links of friendship and support, and offer support to others.

As a group dedicated to achieving a positive change in the world, SGI is also able to have more impact than individuals acting alone, for instance through awareness raising exhibitions or community-based projects.

How does SGI contribute to society?

In the broadest sense, SGI actively promotes peace, culture and education based on a belief in positive human potential and respect for the dignity of life. There are three main levels on which SGI contributes to society. Most significant are the efforts of millions of individual SGI members in their own families, societies and workplaces, where they aim to promote high ideals, help resolve conflict and support the development of capable people. In addition, local SGI groups in individual countries undertake initiatives such as environmental clean-ups, displays and discussions about nonviolence or a culture of peace and cultural exchanges.

At the international level, SGI is a firm supporter of the United Nations, with liaison offices in New York, Geneva and Vienna. It is active in public education with a focus on peace and disarmament, human rights and sustainable development, as well as providing humanitarian assistance in response to natural disasters and participating in interfaith activities. SGI is also engaged in various NGO networks and partnerships at the local, national and international level.

What do SGI members do?

SGI members integrate Buddhist practice into the daily rhythm of their lives. They aim to develop and strengthen their lives through chanting Nam-myoho-renge-kyo and by studying the teachings of Buddhism. The basic morning and evening practice, known as gongyo, consists of chanting Nam-myoho-renge-kyo and reciting portions of the Lotus Sutra. This is usually carried out at home but can also be done together with others.

The aim of this practice is to develop one's Buddha nature--the qualities of courage, wisdom and compassion--thereby tapping the energy needed to tackle one's challenges, transform one's life and contribute to the happiness of others.

In countries where there is an SGI organization, members and guests meet to share experiences of their practice and study together at regular monthly discussion meetings. Practice naturally leads to a sense of empowerment and responsibility, and SGI members aim to positively impact the communities in which they live.

What do Buddhists believe in? What is "enlightenment"?

At the heart of Buddhism lies the belief that each individual has limitless positive potential and the power to change his or her life for the better. Through their practice people can become more fulfilled and happier and also able to contribute more to the world. Buddhism teaches that a universal Law (dharma) underlies everything in the universe, and that all life is interconnected. It also holds that we are all ultimately responsible for determining the direction of our own lives.

Nichiren, a 13th-century Japanese Buddhist priest, formulated the chanting of Nam-myoho-renge-kyo as a practice through which anyone can bring their life into harmony with the dharma or the greater life of the universe, thereby experiencing greater wisdom, courage, life force and compassion.

Enlightenment conjures the image of people practicing austerities in the quest for extraordinary powers beyond the reach of ordinary people. However, Nichiren taught that enlightenment, or Buddhahood, is the fusion of our subjective wisdom with objective reality--a full understanding of the realities of this world. Enlightenment is not a fixed point we someday finally reach. Enlightenment means constant, daily challenge and the renewal of our determination to grow and positively impact the lives of those around us.

In Nichiren's view, enlightenment is not so much a goal or end in itself, as a basis for altruistic action. The life-state of Buddhahood—a condition of limitless vitality, wisdom and compassion—is one which is expressed, maintained and strengthened through committed action to contribute to the well-being and happiness of other people.

How do SGI Buddhists view desires?

Desires are integral to who we are and who we seek to become. Were we to completely rid ourselves of desire, we would undermine our individual and collective will to live. The teachings of Nichiren stress the transformation, rather than the elimination, of desire. Desires and attachments are seen as fuelling the quest for enlightenment. For people living in the midst of ever-changing, stressful realities, those challenges are an effective spur to committed Buddhist practice. Through continuing in Buddhist practice, one's life naturally develops, and desires transform from those that only benefit oneself, and which will only bring transient happiness, to desires that benefit both oneself and others and even the world at large.

Who is a Buddha[10]?

To many, the image conjured up by the word "Buddha" is of an otherworldly being, calmly remote from the matters of this world. Through meditation he has attained state of "nirvana" which will enable him to escape this world and its constant sufferings—the fruit of human delusion and desire.

However, this image does not reflect the truth about the life of Shakyamuni, the founder of Buddhism who lived in India around 2,500 years ago. He was a deeply compassionate man who rejected the extremes of both asceticism and attachment, who was constantly interacting with others and wanted all people to share the truth he had discovered.

The literal meaning of Buddha is "enlightened one." Enlightenment is a fully awakened state of vast wisdom through which reality in all its complexity can be fully understood and enjoyed. Any human being who is awakened to the fundamental truth about life can be called a Buddha.

---

[10] *https://www.sgi.org/about-us/buddhist-concepts/who-is-a-buddha.html*

However, many schools of Buddhism have taught that enlightenment is only accessible after an arduous process undertaken over unimaginably long periods of time—over many lifetimes, in fact. In dramatic contrast, what is considered Shakyamuni's ultimate teaching, the Lotus Sutra, explains that Buddhahood is already present in all life. It teaches absolute equality and emphasizes that even within the life of a person apparently dominated by evil, there exists the unpolished jewel of the Buddha nature. No one else gives it to us or judges whether we "deserve" it.

As with gold hidden in a dirty bag, or lotus flowers emerging from a muddy pond, we have first to believe our Buddha nature is there, then awaken and develop or "polish" it. In Nichiren Buddhism this can be done through devotion to the law contained in the Lotus Sutra and the chanting of the phrase "Nam-myoho-renge-kyo."

But Buddhahood is not a static condition or a state in which one can rest complacently. Rather, it is a dynamic experience and a journey of continual development and discovery.

When we continually reinforce the Buddhahood in our lives, we come to be ruled less and less by selfishness (or greed), anger and foolishness—what Buddhism terms the three poisons. As we fuse our lives with the enlightened life-state of the Buddha, we can tap the potential within us and change ourselves in a fundamental way.

As this inner state of Buddhahood is strengthened, we also develop a fortitude which enables us to ride even the wildest storms. If we are enlightened to the true, unchanging nature of life, we can joyfully surf the waves of difficulty which wash against us in life, creating something of value out of any situation. In this way our "true self" blossoms, and we find vast reserves of courage, compassion, wisdom and energy or life-force inside us. We find ourselves becoming more active and feeling deep inner freedom. And as we experience a growing sense of oneness with the universe, the isolation and alienation that cause so much suffering evaporate. We lessen our attachment to our smaller egotistical self, to difference, and become aware instead of the interconnectedness of all life. Gradually we find our lives opening up to those of others, desiring their happiness as much as our own.

However, while it is easy to believe that we all possess the lower life-states outlined in Buddhist teachings (hell, hunger, animality, anger and so on), believing that we possess Buddhahood is much more difficult. But the struggle to develop and constantly strengthen this state within our lives is well worthwhile.

For, in the words of SGI President Daisaku Ikeda, "[Buddhahood] is the joy of joys. Birth, old age, illness and death are no longer suffering, but part of the joy of living. The light of wisdom illuminates the entire universe, casting back the innate darkness of life. The life-space of the Buddha becomes united and fused with the universe. The self becomes the cosmos, and in a single instant the life-flow stretches out to encompass all that is past and all that is future. In each moment of the present, the eternal life-force of the cosmos pours forth as a gigantic fountain of energy."

How does chanting Nam-myoho-renge-kyo work?

SGI members often speak about the positive impact that chanting Nam-myoho-renge-kyo has on their lives. This is hard to comprehend and is something that can only be experienced on an individual basis.

Often people trying the practice are encouraged to try chanting even a small amount regularly for a while, in order to see the effect it has. The 13th-century priest Nichiren established the practice of chanting Nam-myoho-renge-kyo. He concluded that the Lotus Sutra contains the full truth of Buddhism: that everyone without exception has the potential to attain Buddhahood.

The title of the Lotus Sutra in its Japanese translation is Myoho-renge-kyo. By chanting "Nam," or devotion to the essential message of the Lotus Sutra, we activate the state of Buddhahood in our lives. Rather than being a prayer to an external being, chanting Nam-myoho-renge-kyo is an expression of the determination of the human spirit, seeking to come into rhythm with the reality of the universe. Through continuing in this practice of determined intention we bring forth our highest potential from within our lives.

What is Daisaku Ikeda's role as president of the SGI?

Daisaku Ikeda writes essays, articles and books on the Buddhist philosophy of Nichiren and the Lotus Sutra to inspire and encourage the members of SGI around the world. His focus is on making profound Buddhist truths applicable to daily life. Several times a month he meets with SGI and Soka Gakkai members to share his perspectives and encourage them in their efforts to put Buddhism into practice. His focus is often on youth, as he is always concerned with passing on what he has learned. He also meets and corresponds with leading figures to discuss global issues and ways of building a more peaceful world.

What are his core beliefs?

Daisaku Ikeda believes in the positive potential of human beings and that it is possible for us to coexist in peace as well as in harmony with our environment. He holds that sustained dialogue can bridge the gaps which divide us. He believes that vast possibility for creating a better world can be sparked by the inner change or "human revolution" of even a single person. Ikeda's beliefs are based on the core principles of Nichiren Buddhism and the Mahayana tradition as expressed in the Lotus Sutra. These principles include:

The oneness of life and its environment
The oneness of body and mind
The interconnectedness of all life
The eternity of life
That each individual is responsible for their own destiny
The value of diversity and preciousness of each unique individual
That the greatest happiness is found in working for the happiness of others.

How has Daisaku Ikeda contributed to peace?

Born in Tokyo in 1928, Daisaku Ikeda experienced first-hand the horror of war. He determined to devote himself to building peace, and particularly to healing relations between Japan and China. For over 50 years, he has also consistently taken action toward the abolition of nuclear weapons, organizing petition drives, issuing proposals and writing articles to that end.

Ikeda's efforts to build peace range from citizen diplomacy during the Cold War, particularly helping to lessen tensions between China and the USSR, to ongoing dialogues aimed at increasing mutual understanding with a wide range of people from around the world--over 50 of his dialogues have been published in book form.

As president of SGI, Ikeda has also issued annual peace proposals since 1983 containing ideas grounded in Buddhist humanism for viable responses to global issues. Ikeda has also established several institutions promoting peace, humanistic education and cultural exchange.

Why do SGI members regard him as their mentor?

Many SGI members view Daisaku Ikeda as their mentor due to the depth of his understanding of Buddhism and his exceptional scholarship. His continuous efforts to encourage others to deepen their understanding and become empowered through the philosophy and practice of Buddhism also awaken a response.

Ikeda often stresses how he owes everything to his own teacher or mentor, second Soka Gakkai President Josei Toda (1900-58), who in turn regarded Tsunesaburo Makiguchi (1871-1944), the founder of the Soka Gakkai, as his mentor.

The tradition of passing down teachings from mentor to disciple, or teacher to student, has a long history in Buddhism. The commitment of the mentor, or teacher, is solely to passing on what he or she has learned and encouraging the development of the disciple, or pupil, so that eventually the disciple surpasses the mentor. In this way the continual development of Buddhism is assured.

SGI members speak of the shared commitment of mentor and disciple to spreading the peaceful principles of Buddhism throughout the world. More than any theoretical explanation, it is through the life-to-life connection of the mentor-disciple relationship that people can gain encouragement and develop their ability to overcome the challenges they face.

Why does SGI stress individual empowerment?

Buddhism emphasizes the possibility of inner transformation--a process of bringing forth our full human potential. There is a common perception that the discipline and focus necessary for such a process requires a set of ideal circumstances not available to most. Nichiren Buddhism, however, teaches that it is only by squarely facing the challenges that confront us amidst the harsh contradictions of society that we can change our own lives and the world for the better. While the role of institutions or governments is important, change that starts within each person's life is seen the surest way to tackle the problems facing the world in the 21st century. Many people feel hopeless about these issues, but SGI stresses that people have the power to change their circumstances, and its public education and outreach projects aim to inspire people and equip them with information that they can use to make a difference in their communities.

How does SGI cooperate with other religious groups?

SGI organizations around the world, from Singapore to Australia and Spain, are engaged in interfaith dialogue and cooperation, believing that it is important for faith groups to find common ground and work together to resolve the complex issues facing humanity. SGI members regularly participate in the Parliament of the World's Religions and other interfaith forums. SGI's representative to the UN in New York served as president of the Committee of Religious NGOs at the UN from 2004 to 2007.

Does SGI engage in political lobbying?

As an NGO, SGI is engaged in concrete constructive efforts to promote nuclear abolition, human rights education and education for sustainable development, in cooperation with other NGOs and UN agencies. For unique historical reasons, the Soka Gakkai in Japan is the main endorsing body for the New Komeito Party, which has a platform of policies aimed at peace, environmental protection and support for the vulnerable. For more information on the nature of the relationship between New Komeito and Soka Gakkai see www.sokaissues.info/home/why-politics.html. SGI organizations outside Japan do not engage in political activities.

How do I start practicing Nichiren Buddhism[11]?

"Just chant Nam-myoho-renge-kyo"

Anyone can start practising Nichiren Buddhism by having faith in the Gohonzon and chanting the phrase, "Nam-myoho-renge-kyo" (chanting means reciting this phrase repeatedly).

You can chant at some Soka centres which are open at stipulated time for prayers. You can also chant at home facing the east (direction of the sunrise). If you do not have the Gohonzon to pray to, just visualize the Gohonzon in your mind as you chant.

How long you chant depends entirely on you. Of course, the more you chant, the greater will be the benefits accruing from your sincere prayers. For new friends who just begin their practice, you may start by chanting 5 or 15 minutes and increasing the period to half, one or more hours as you become more comfortable with the practice. Before you end the chanting, offer your silent prayers, this means to express your wishes to the Gohonzon silently in your heart.

Later you may also learn to recite the 2 important chapters of Lotus Sutra.

[1111] https://ssabuddhist.org/philosophy-and-practice/faq/#.XMwLgehKhPY

I find it hard to empty my mind. Can I still be a Buddhist?

Yes. To have many things on our minds, even during our Buddhist practice, is human. The goal of practice in the SGI is to strengthen our positive qualities and create value in life. Through chanting Nam-myoho-renge-kyo, we naturally develop the ability to focus and to see ourselves and our own minds more clearly. We are then better able to direct them in the most constructive direction.

Nichiren speaks of the need to "Become the master of your mind rather than let your mind master you." Calming the mind may come as one benefit from chanting but it is not a prerequisite and it is not the goal of the practice. The aim is to tap the vitality, wisdom and compassion innate within us, and apply those qualities to how we live. The goal of Buddhism is to win in life and contribute to the happiness of others--both pursuits needing constructive thought and action.

How can I find a local meeting?
Please visit: https://www.sgi.org/contact-us/

Printed in Great Britain
by Amazon